Carnival

Colouring Book

Adult Coloring Books

Aryla Publishing 2019

978-1-912675-34-0

www.arylapublishing.com

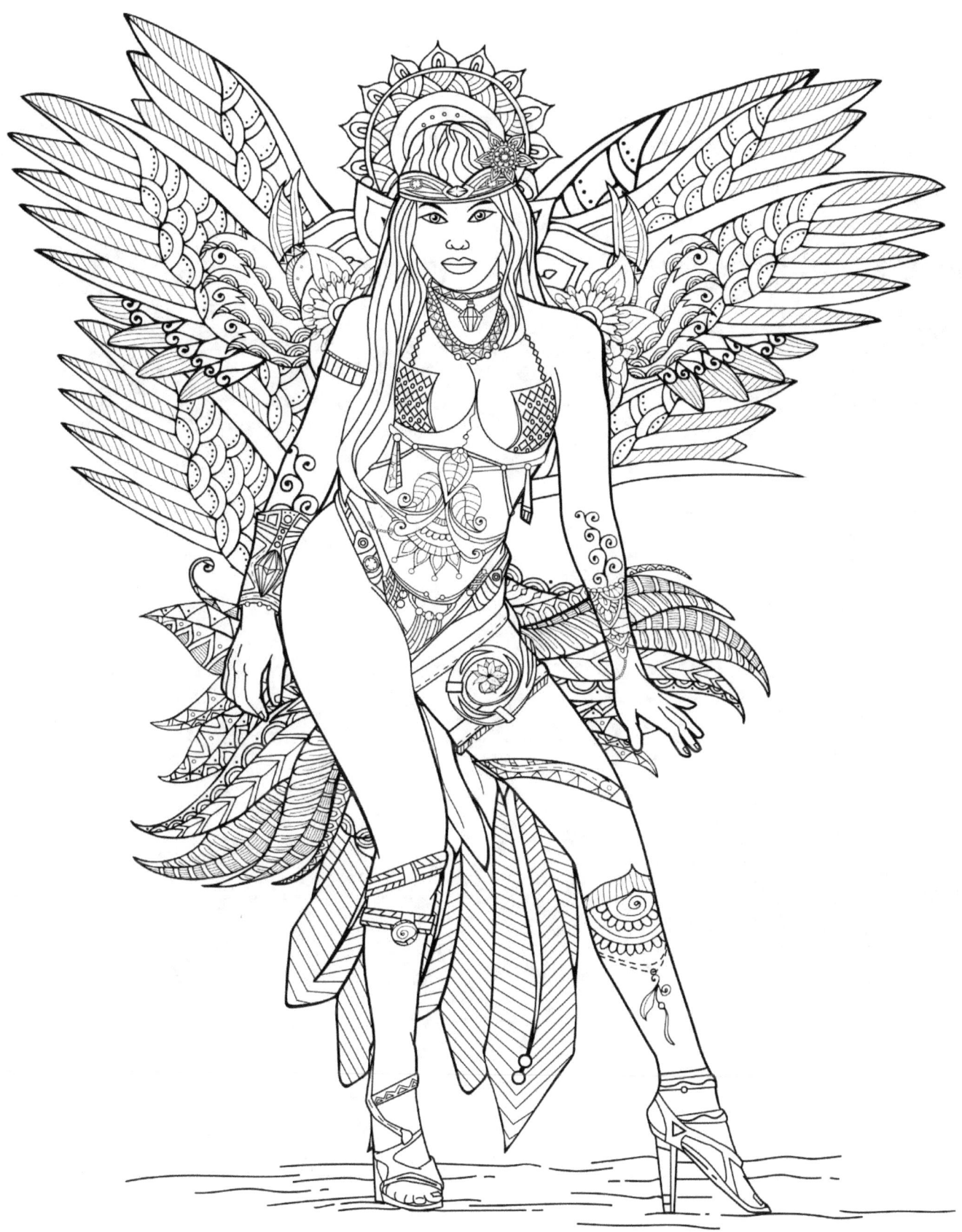

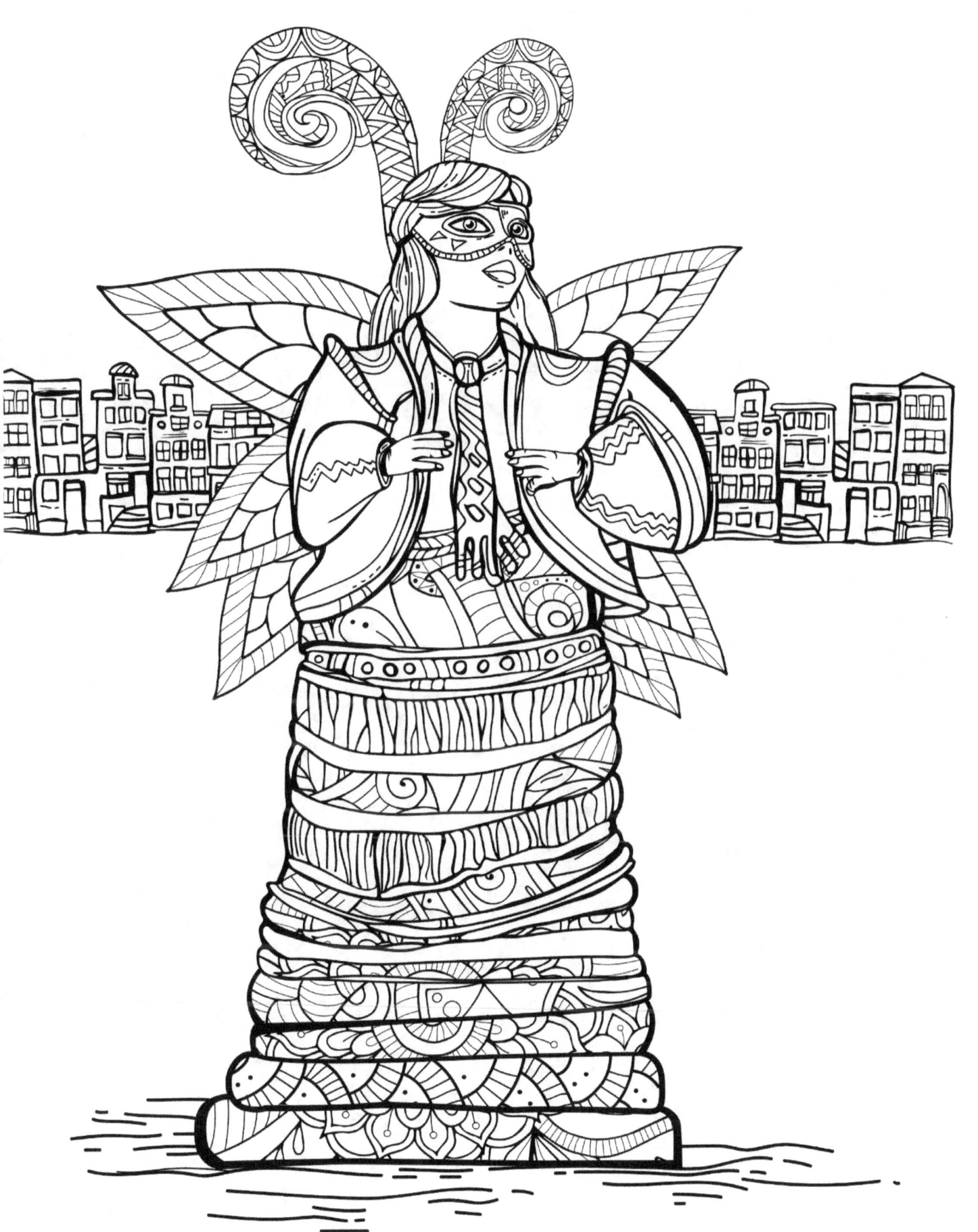

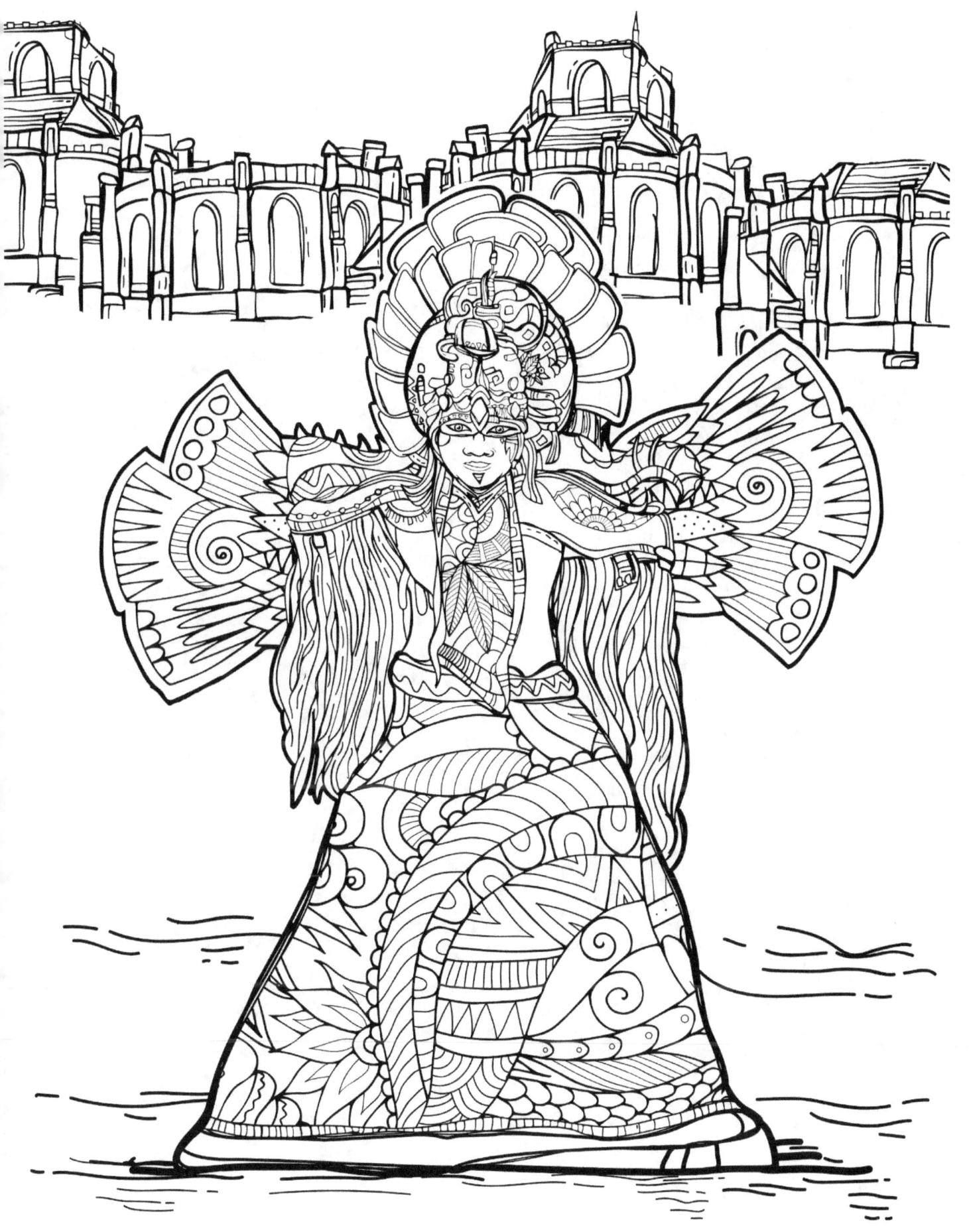

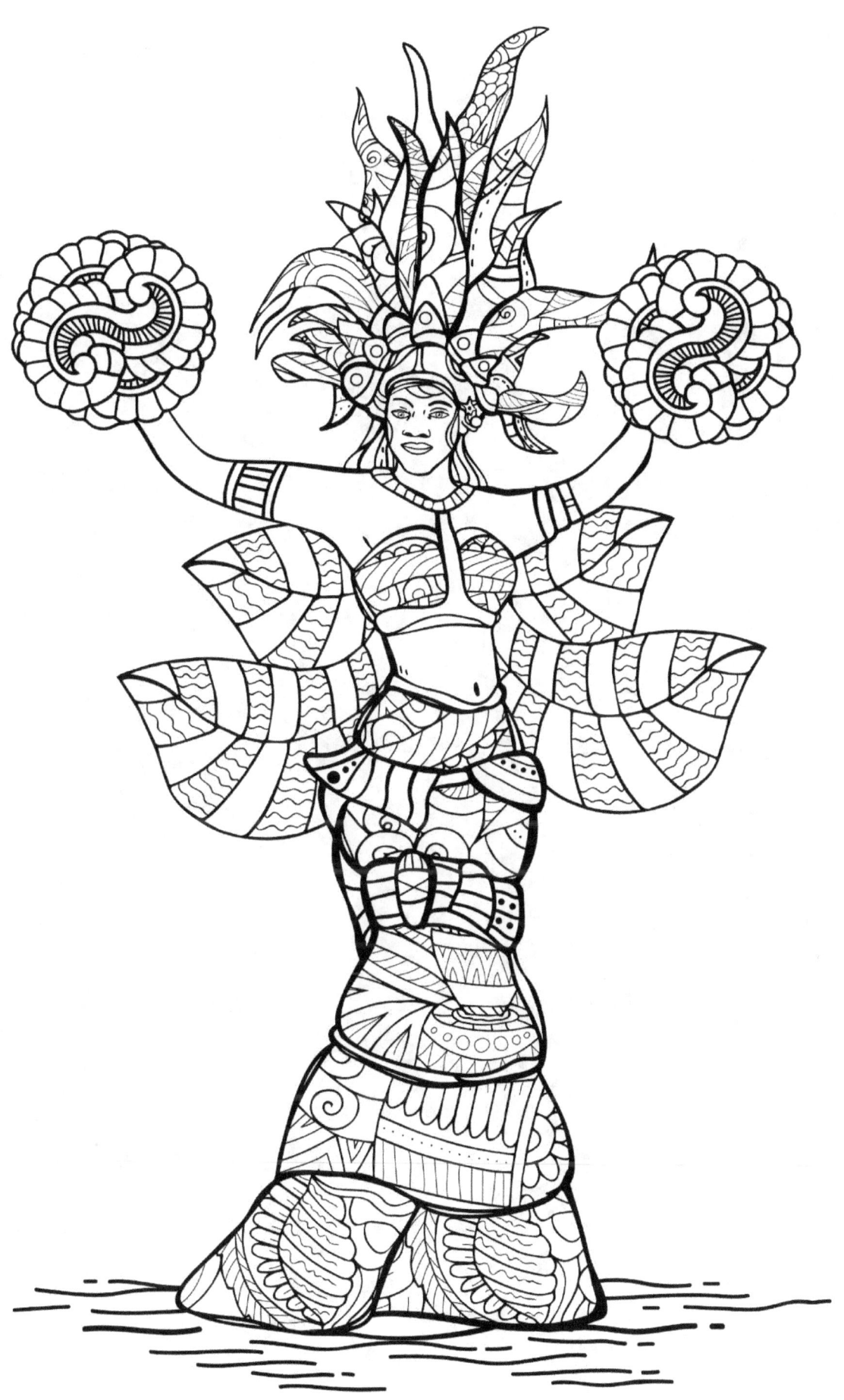

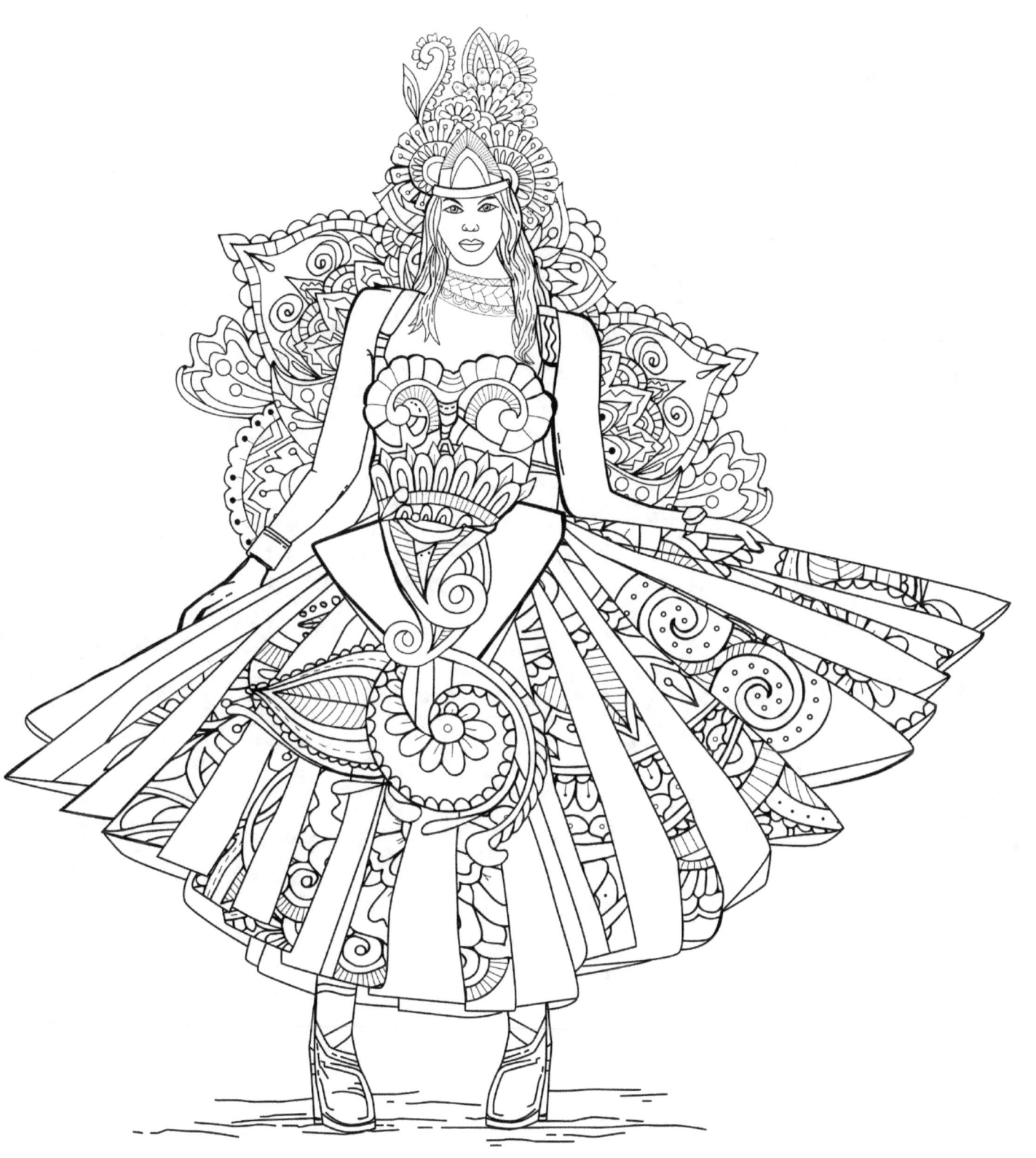

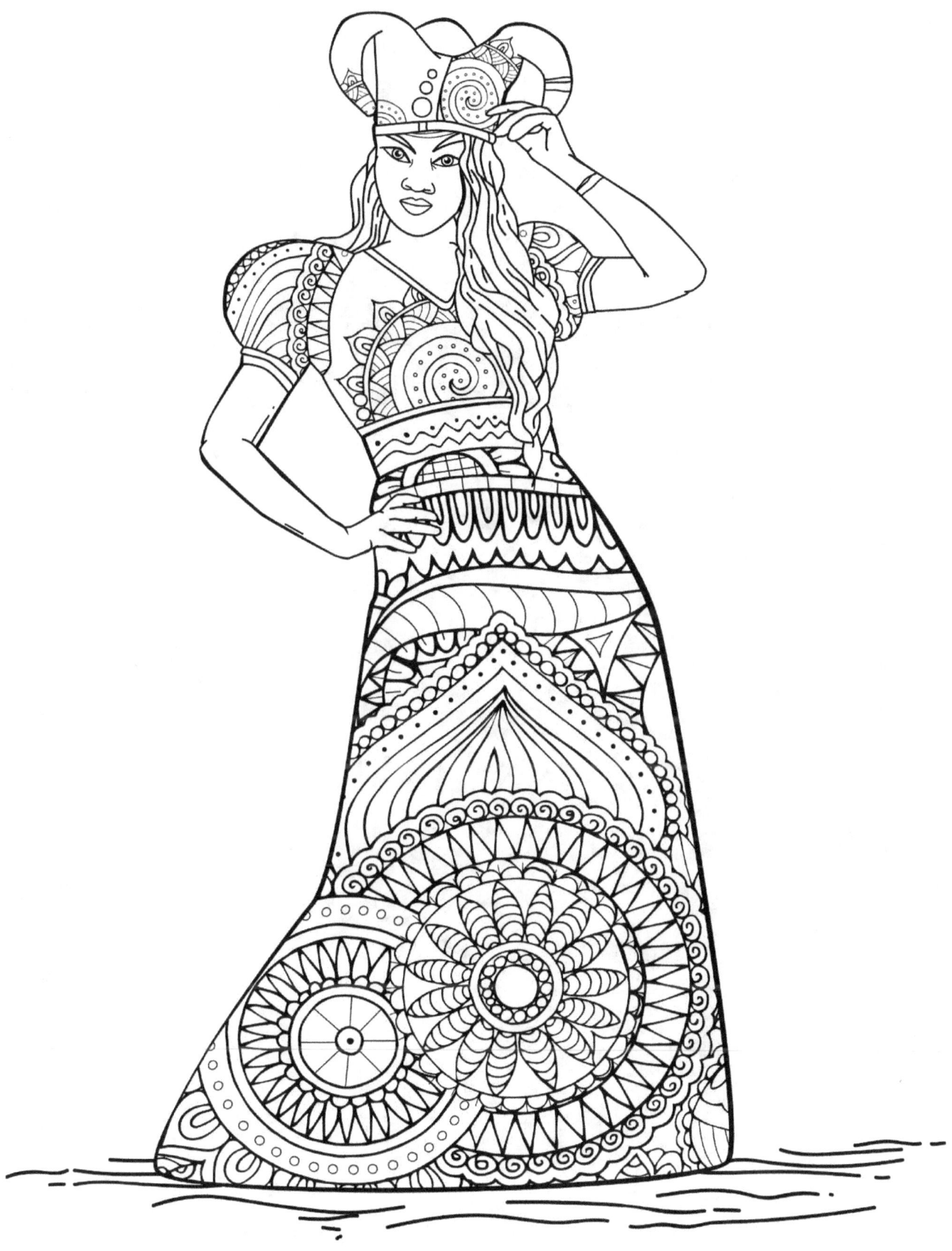

Día de los Muertos

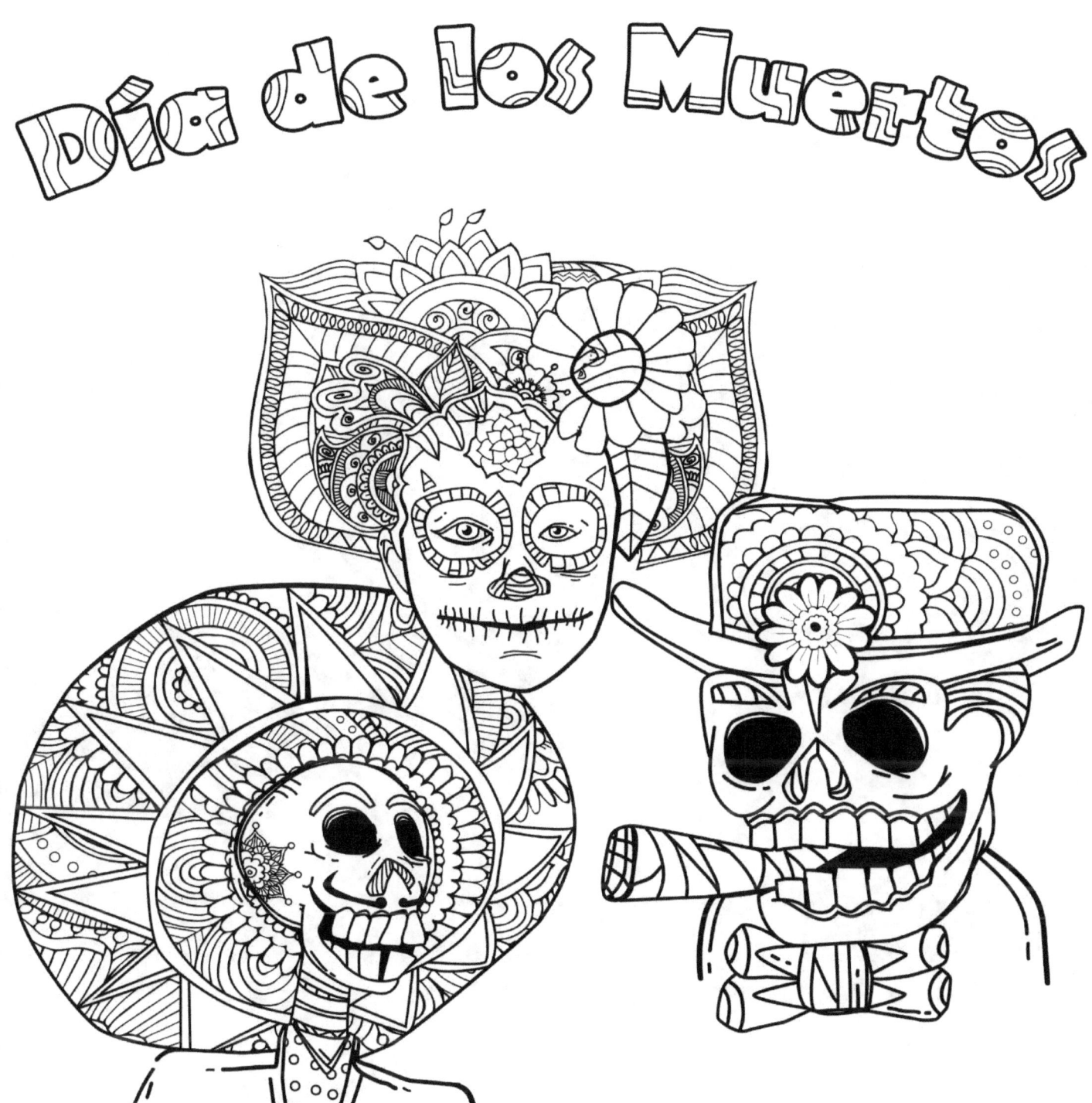

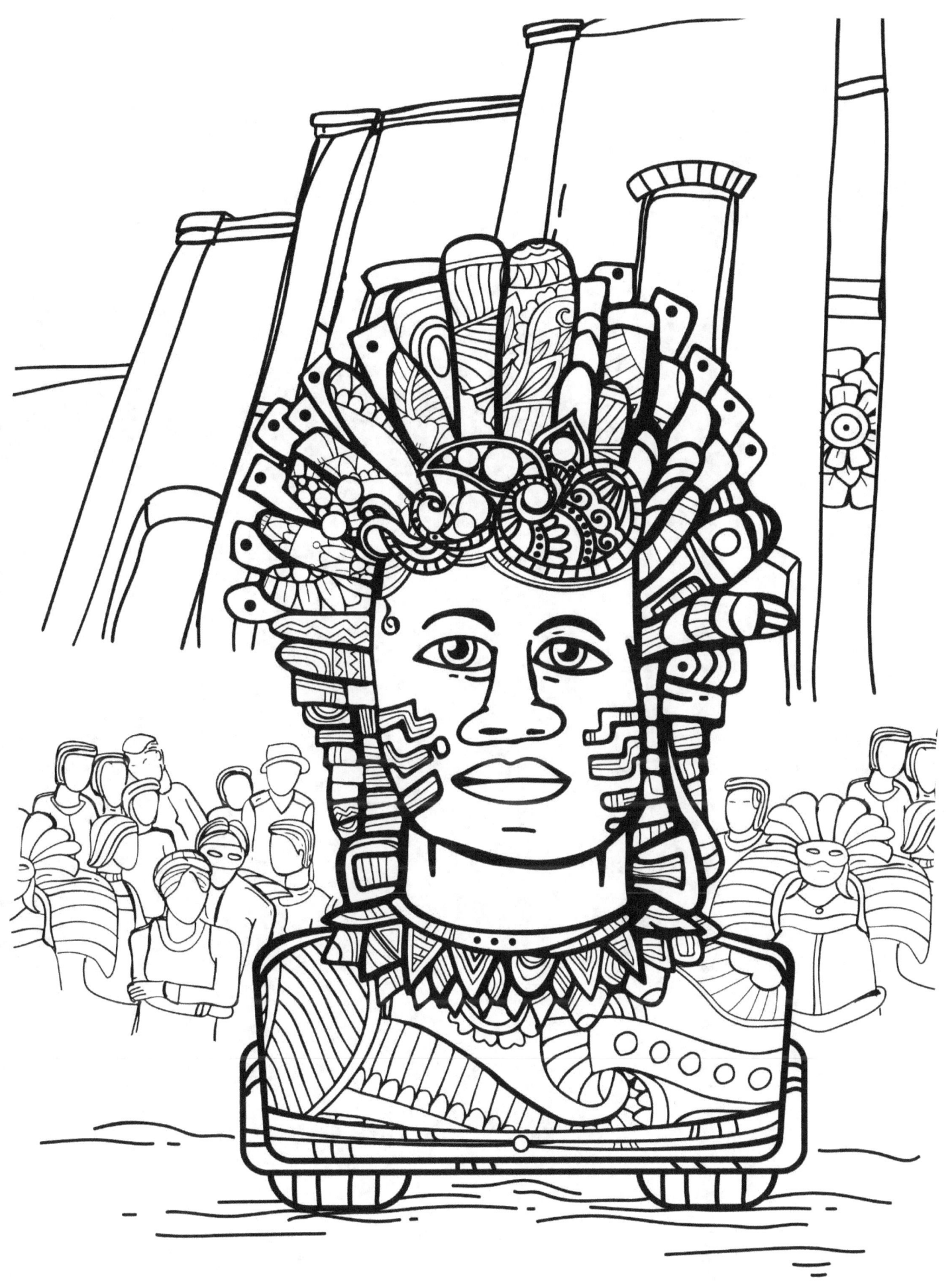

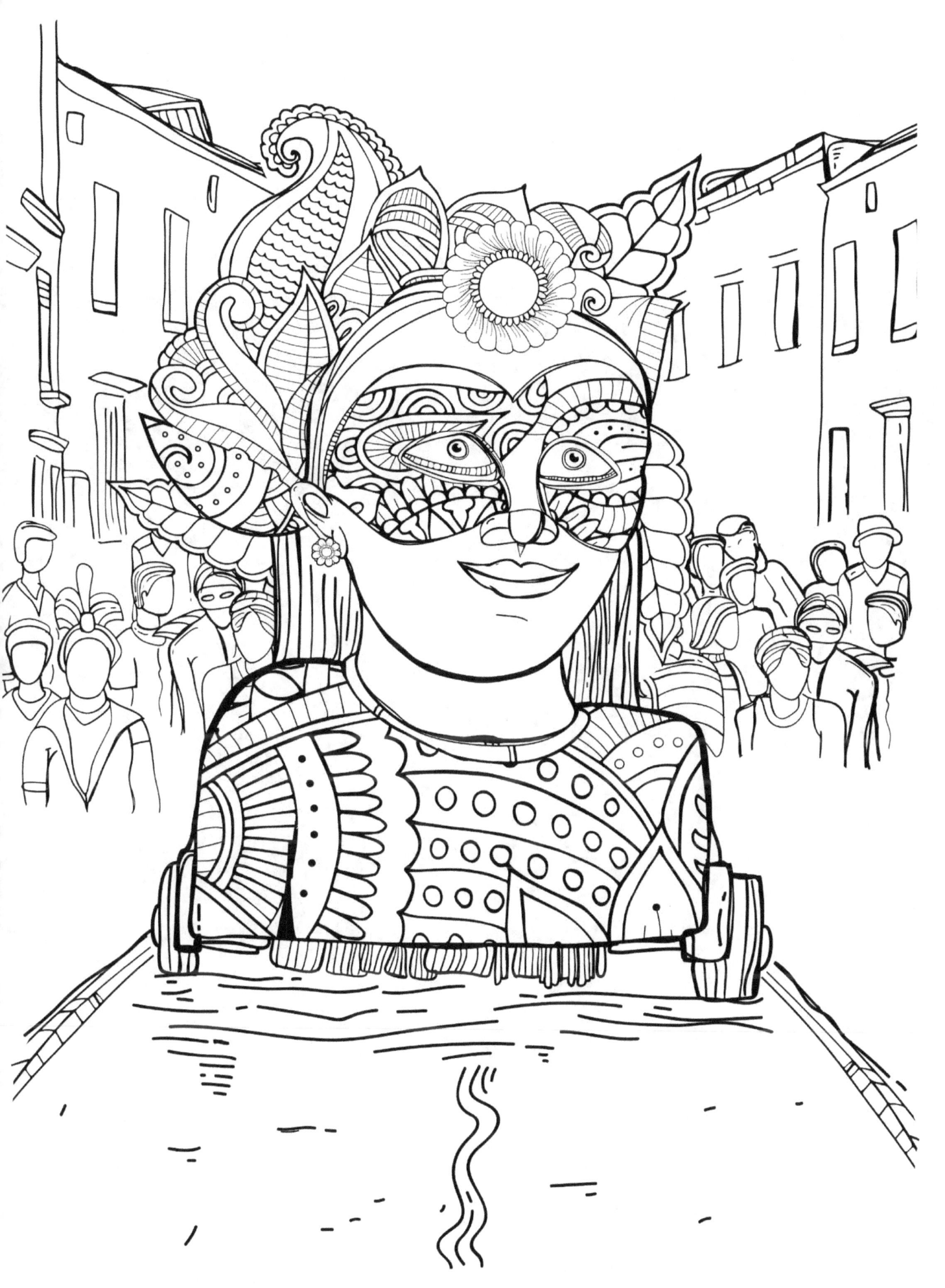

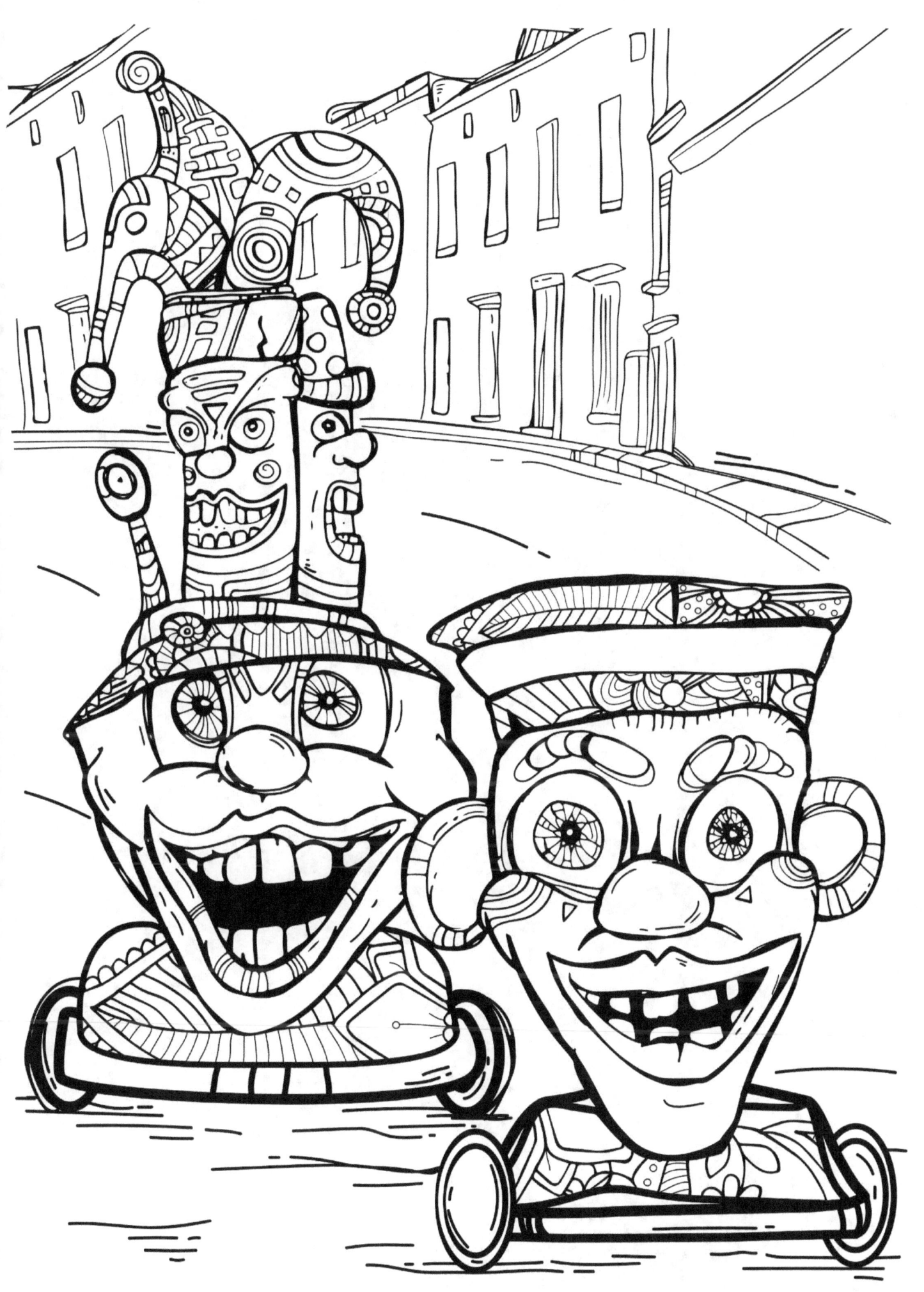

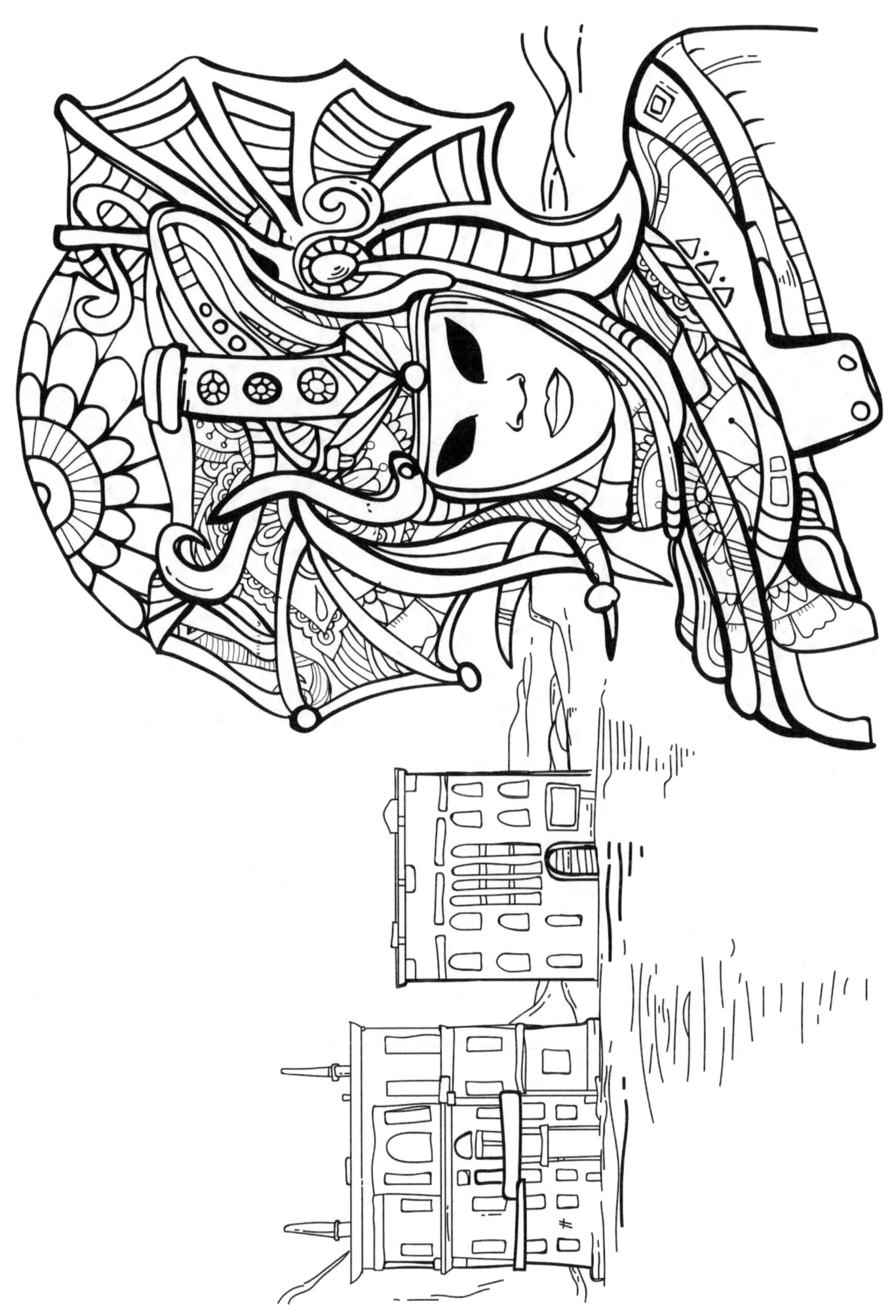

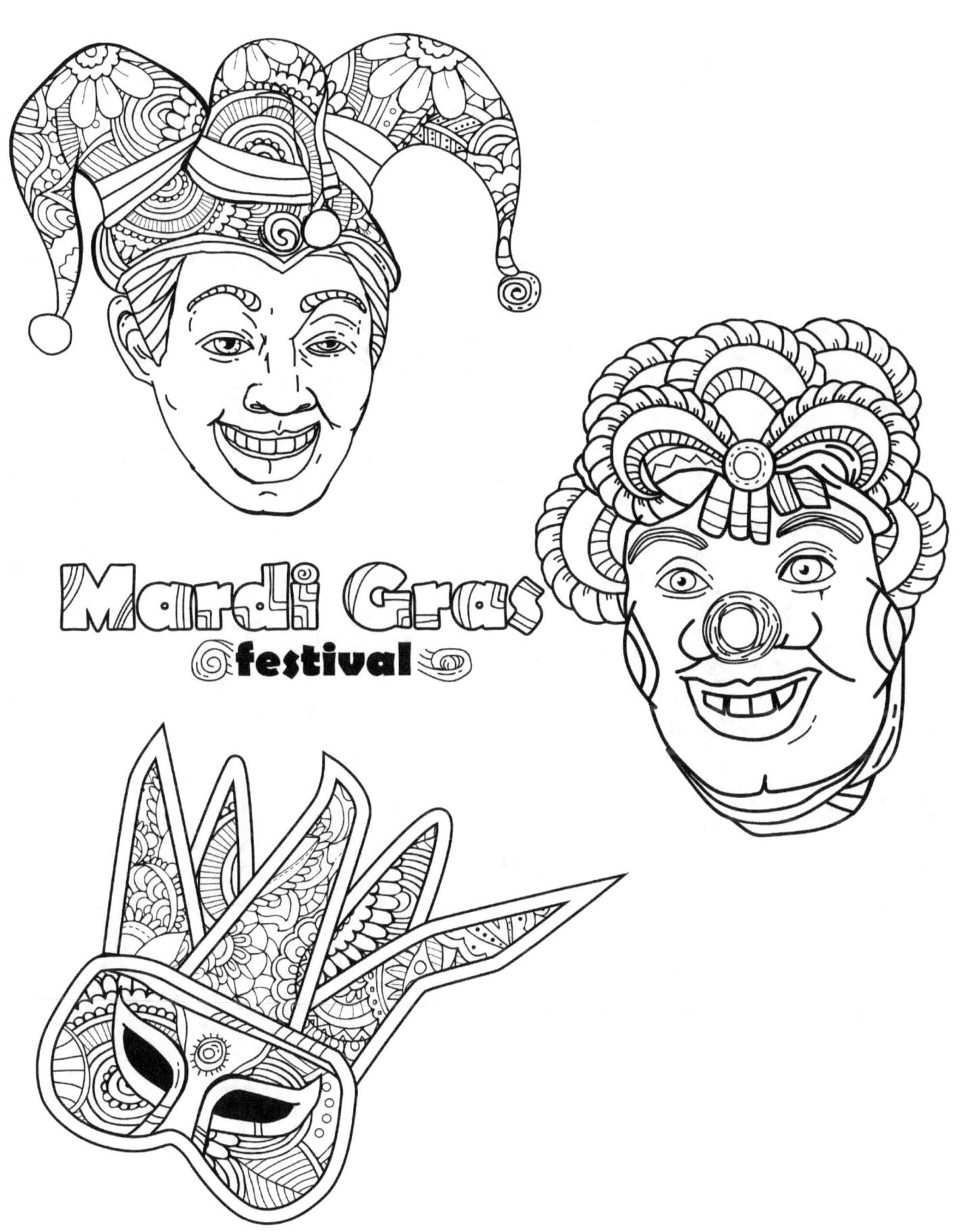

Mardi Gras festival

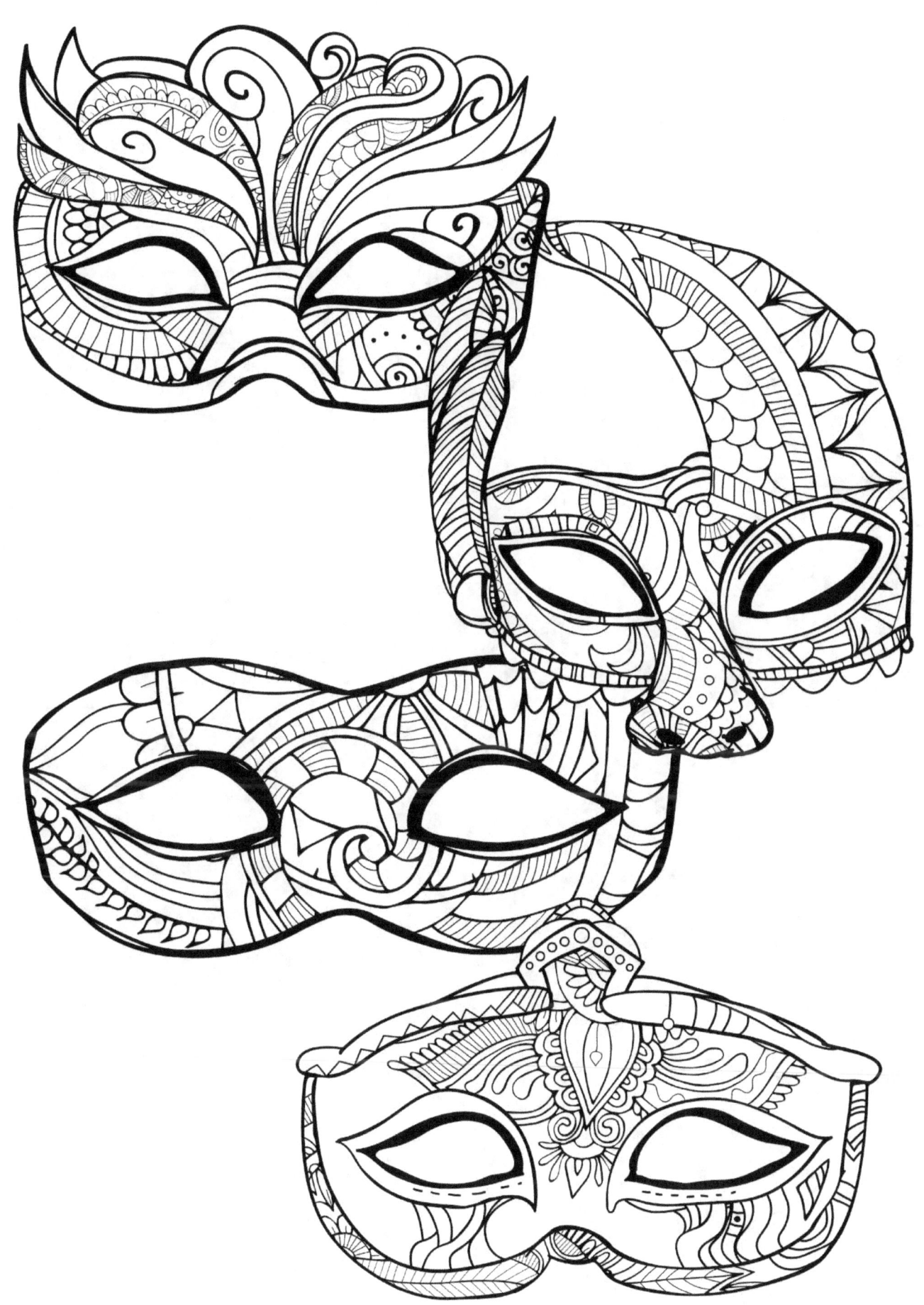

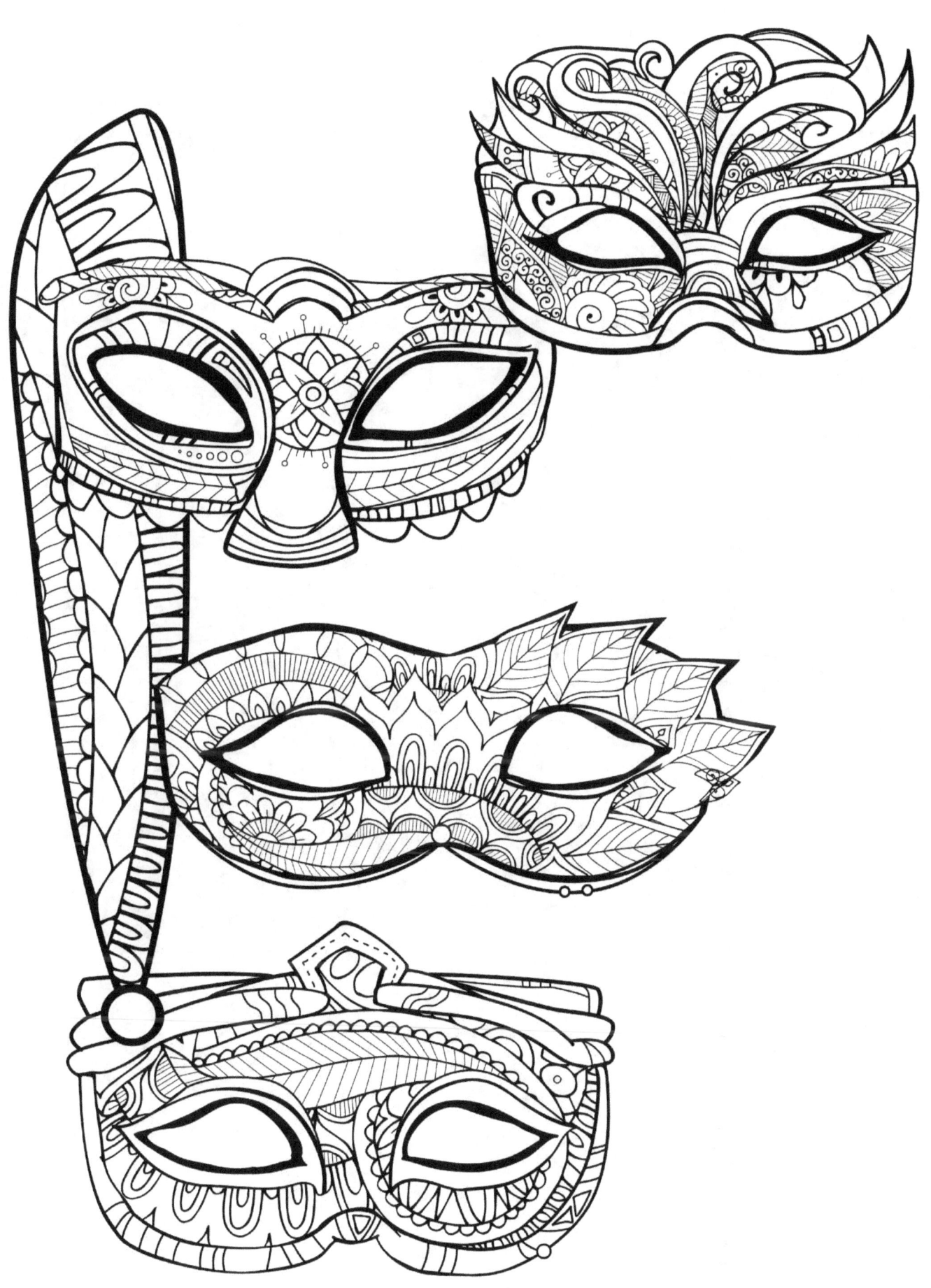

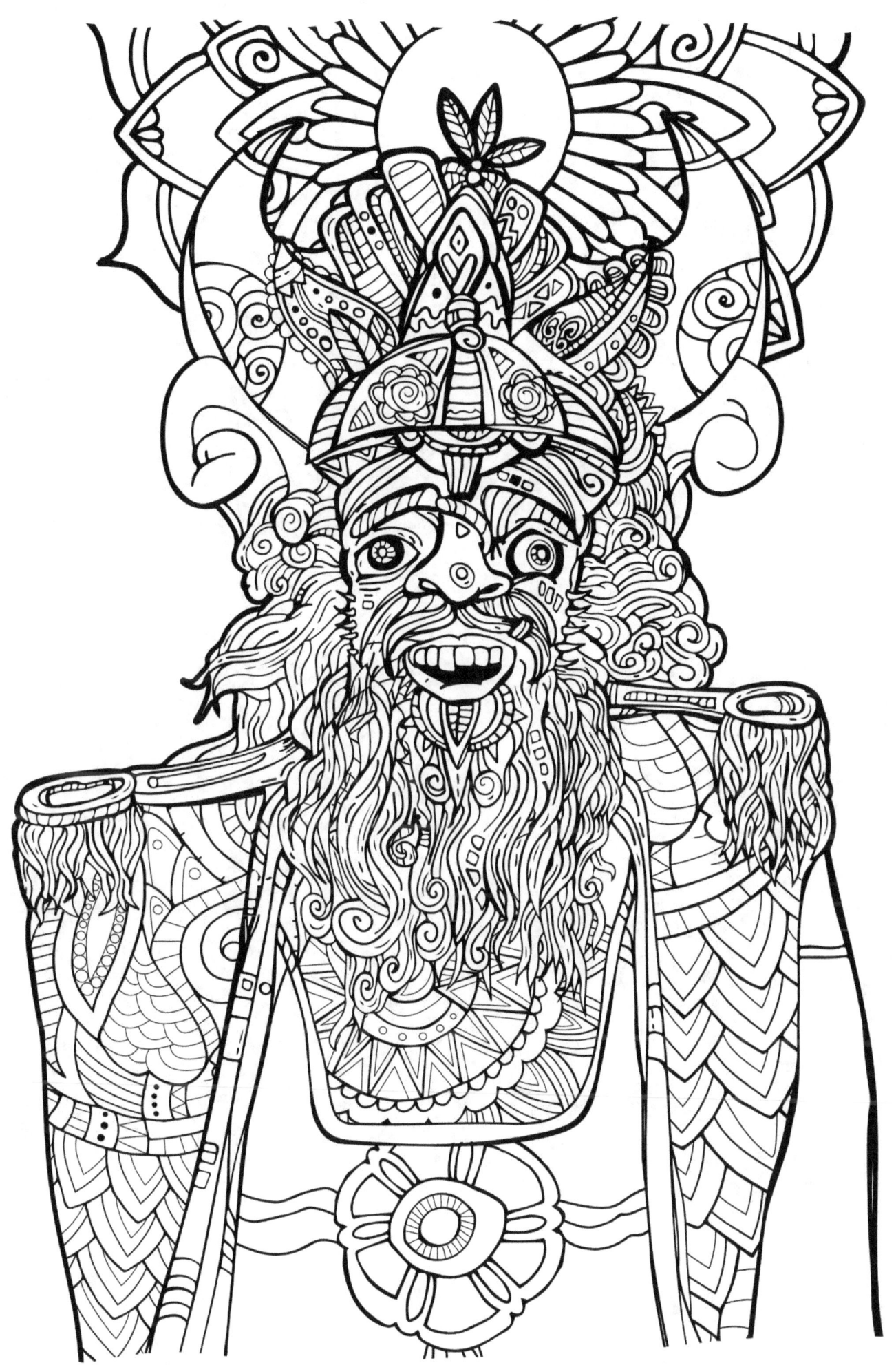

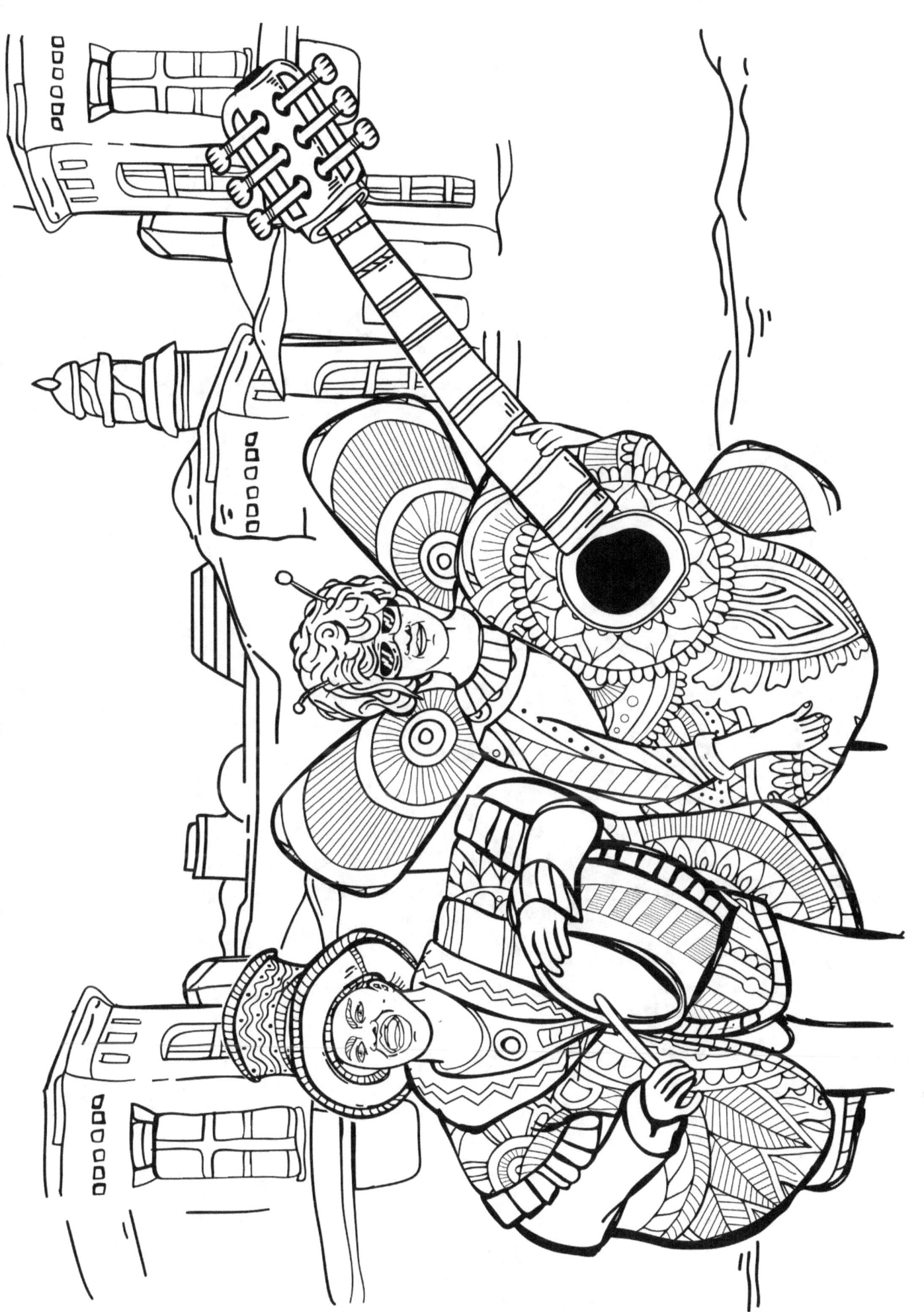

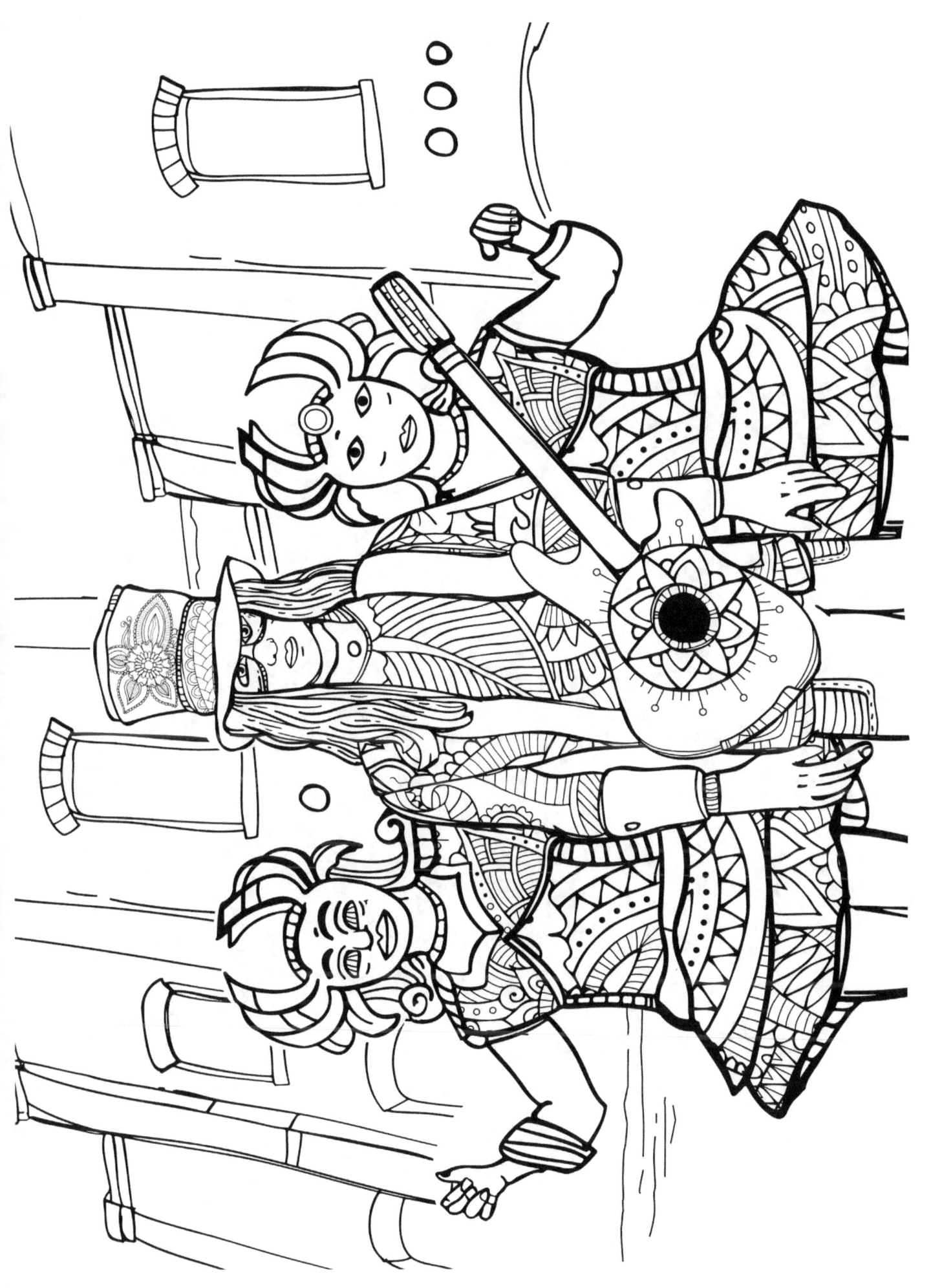

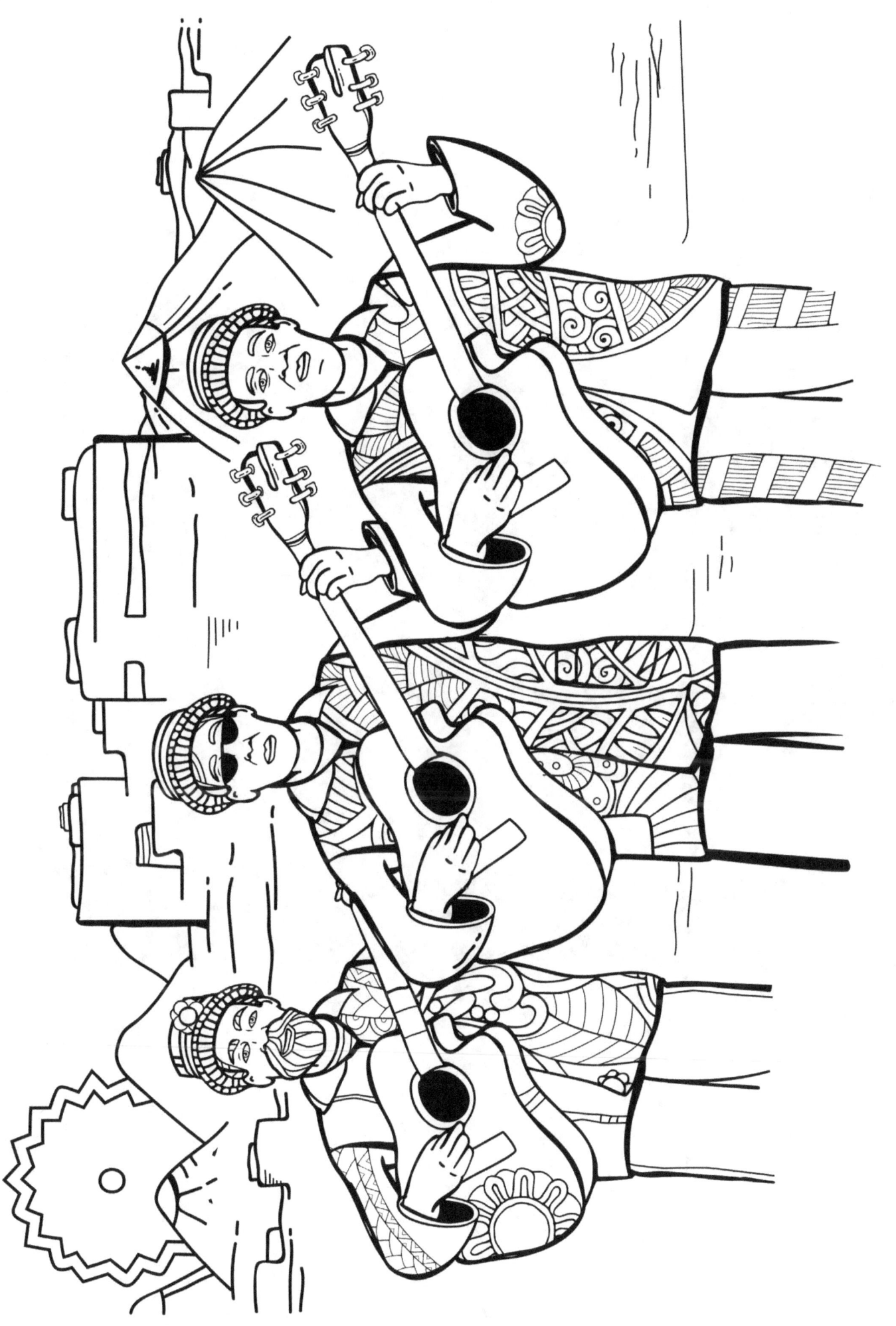

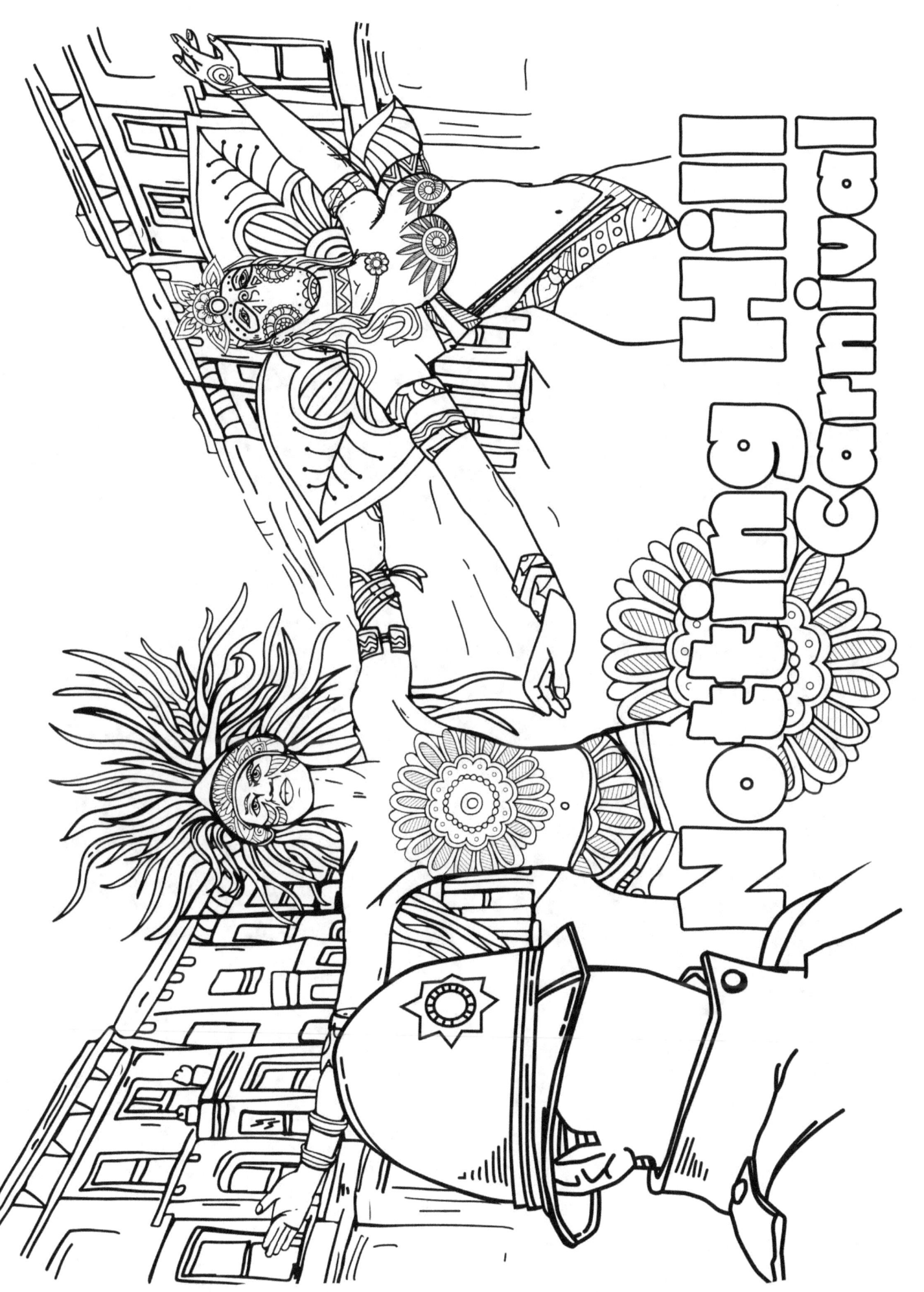

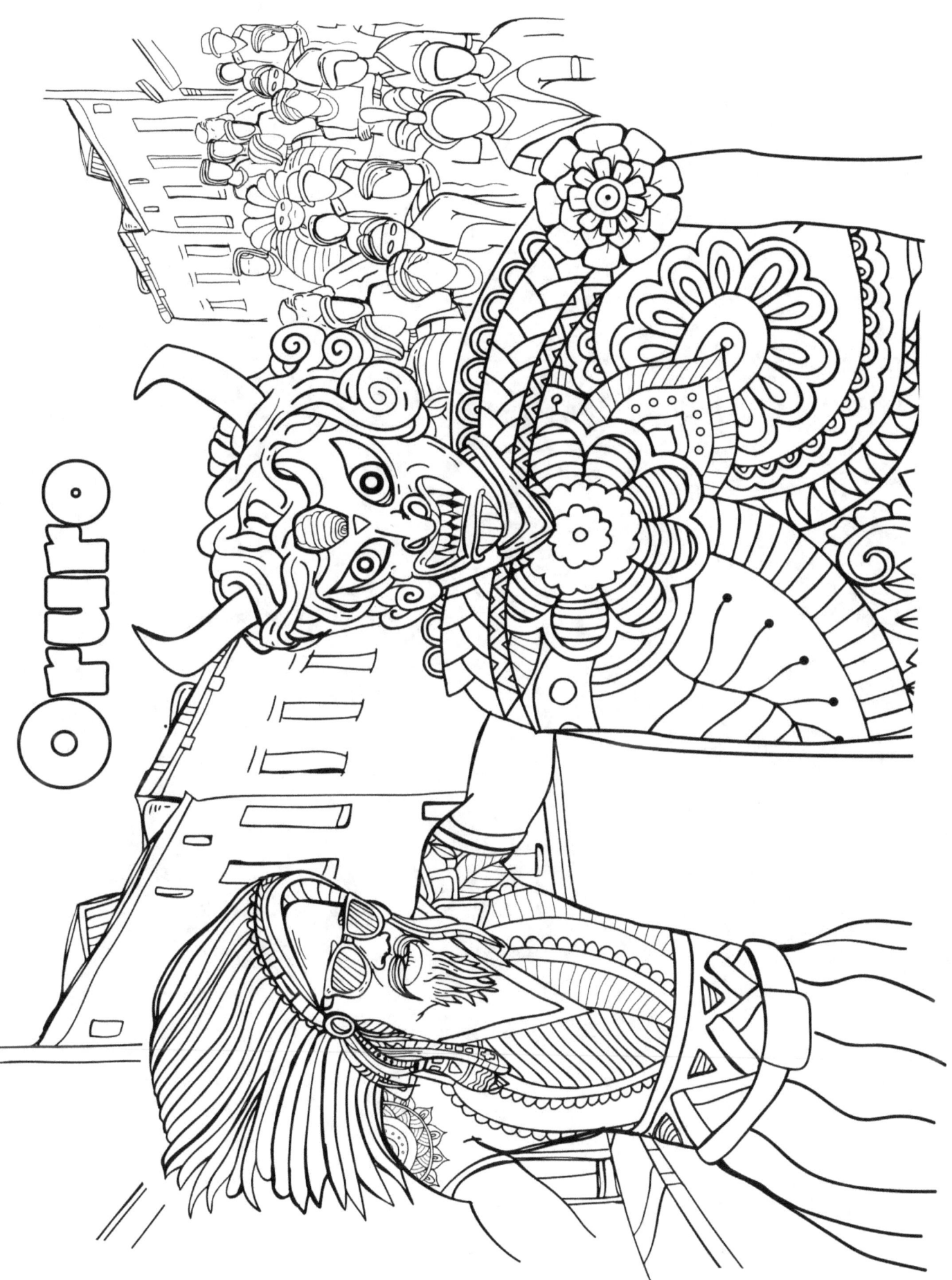

Oruro

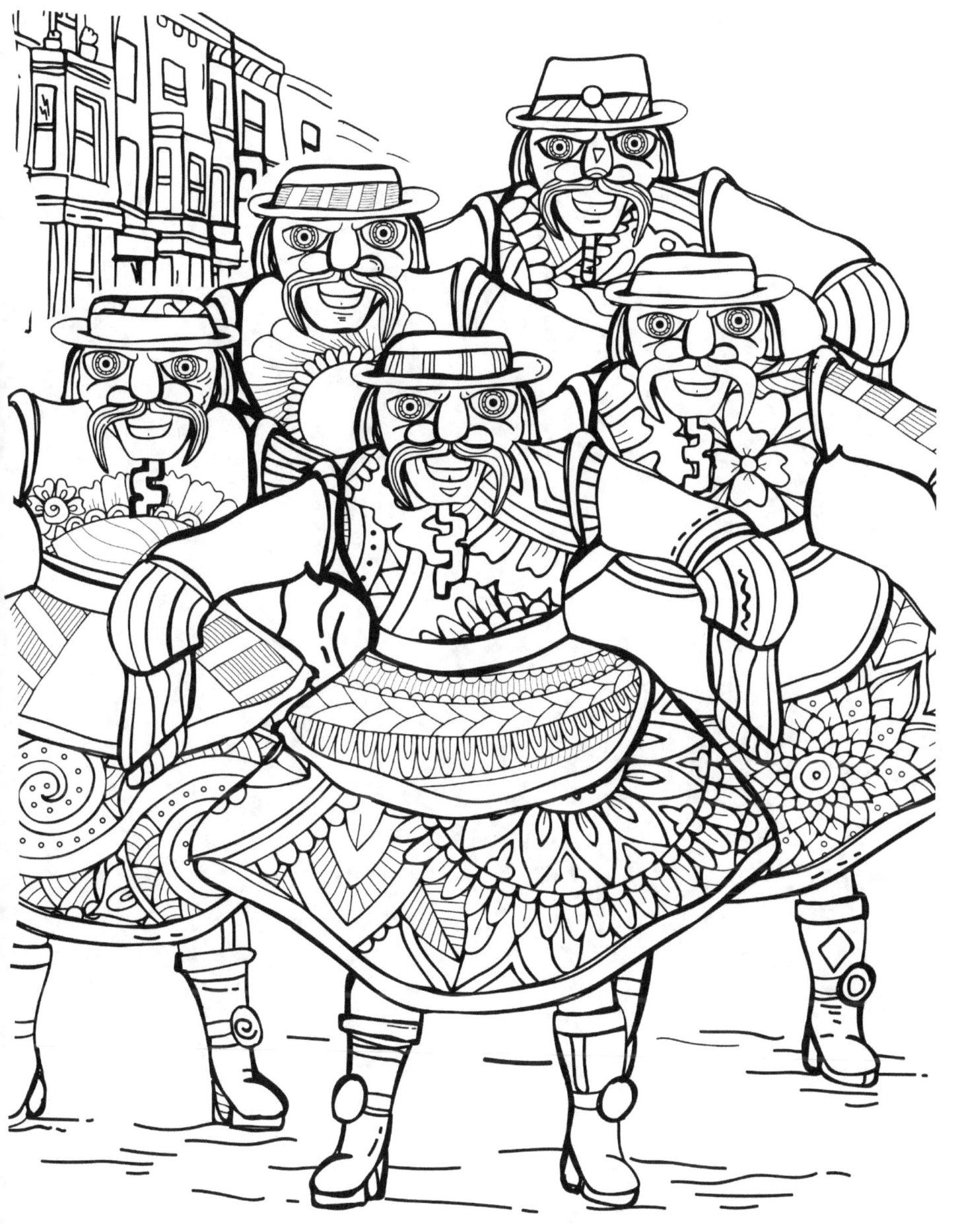

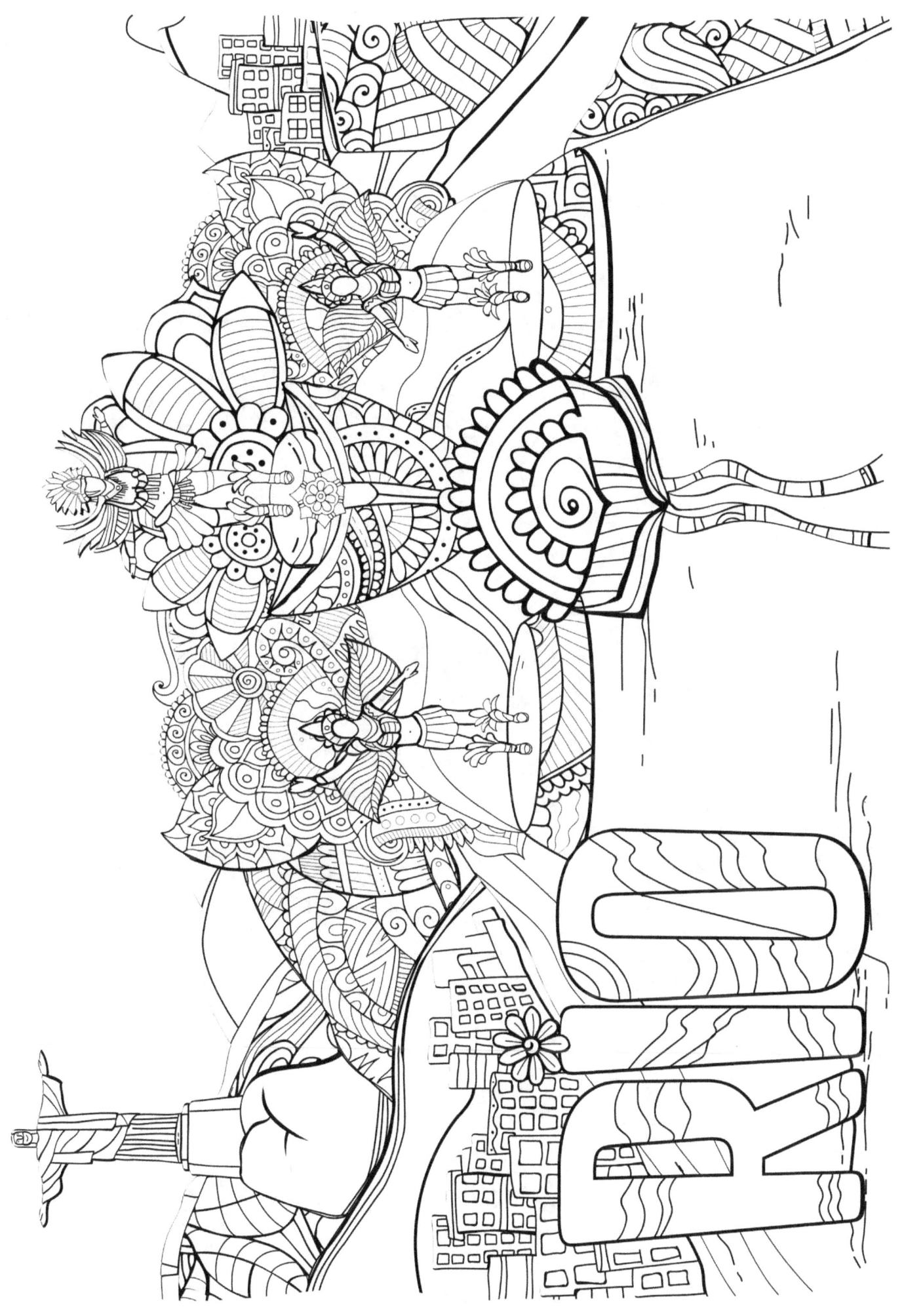

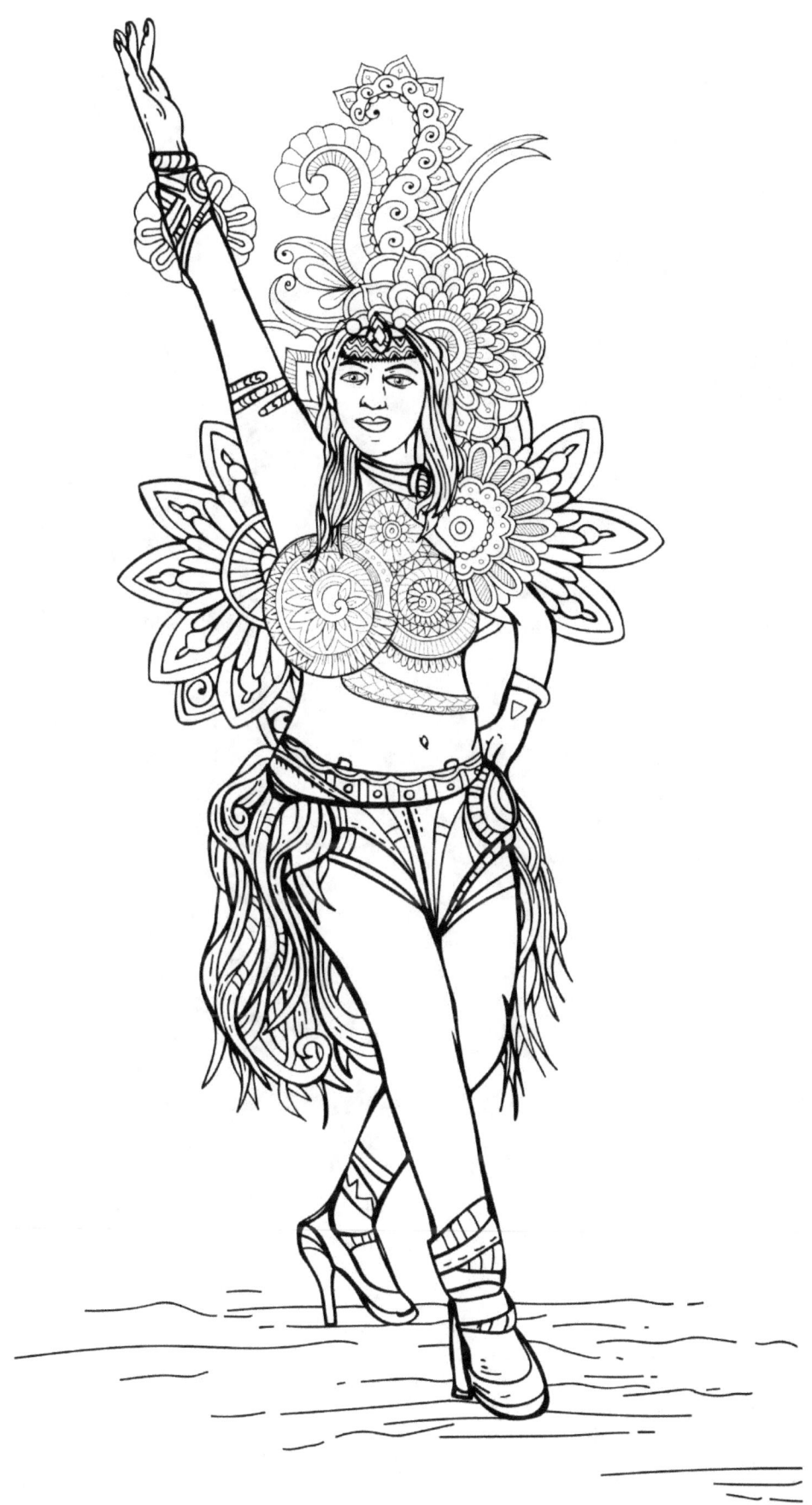

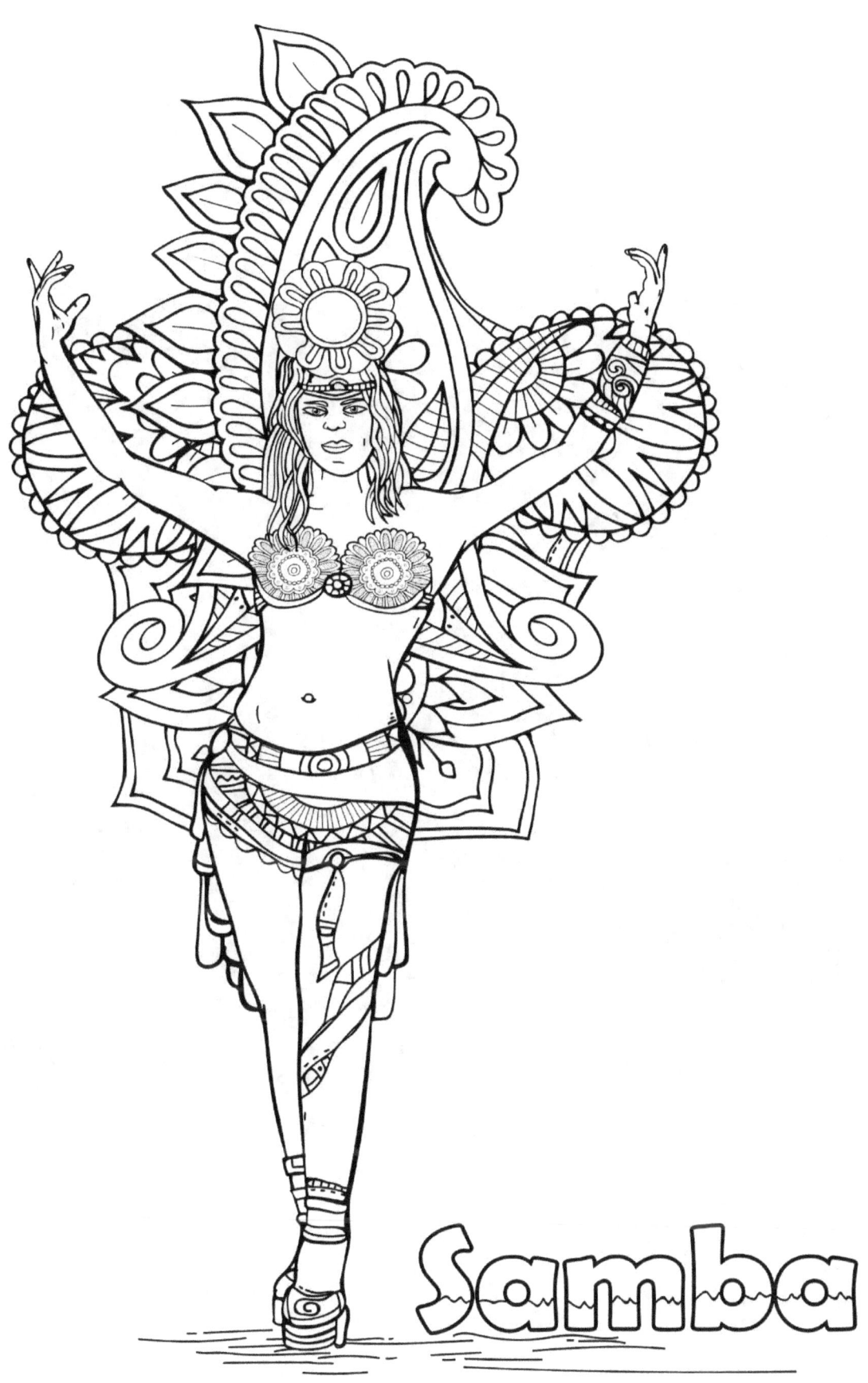

Samba

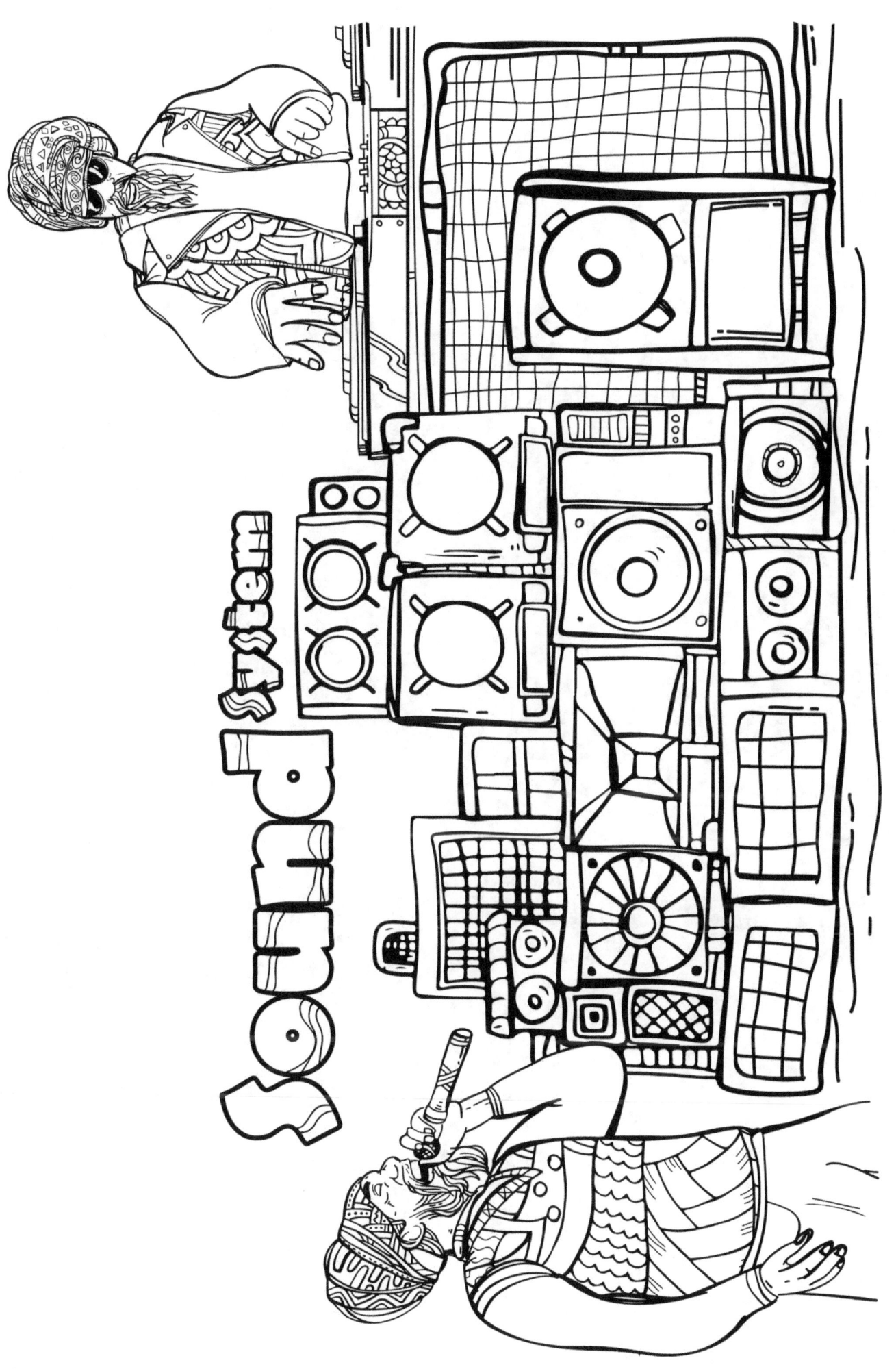

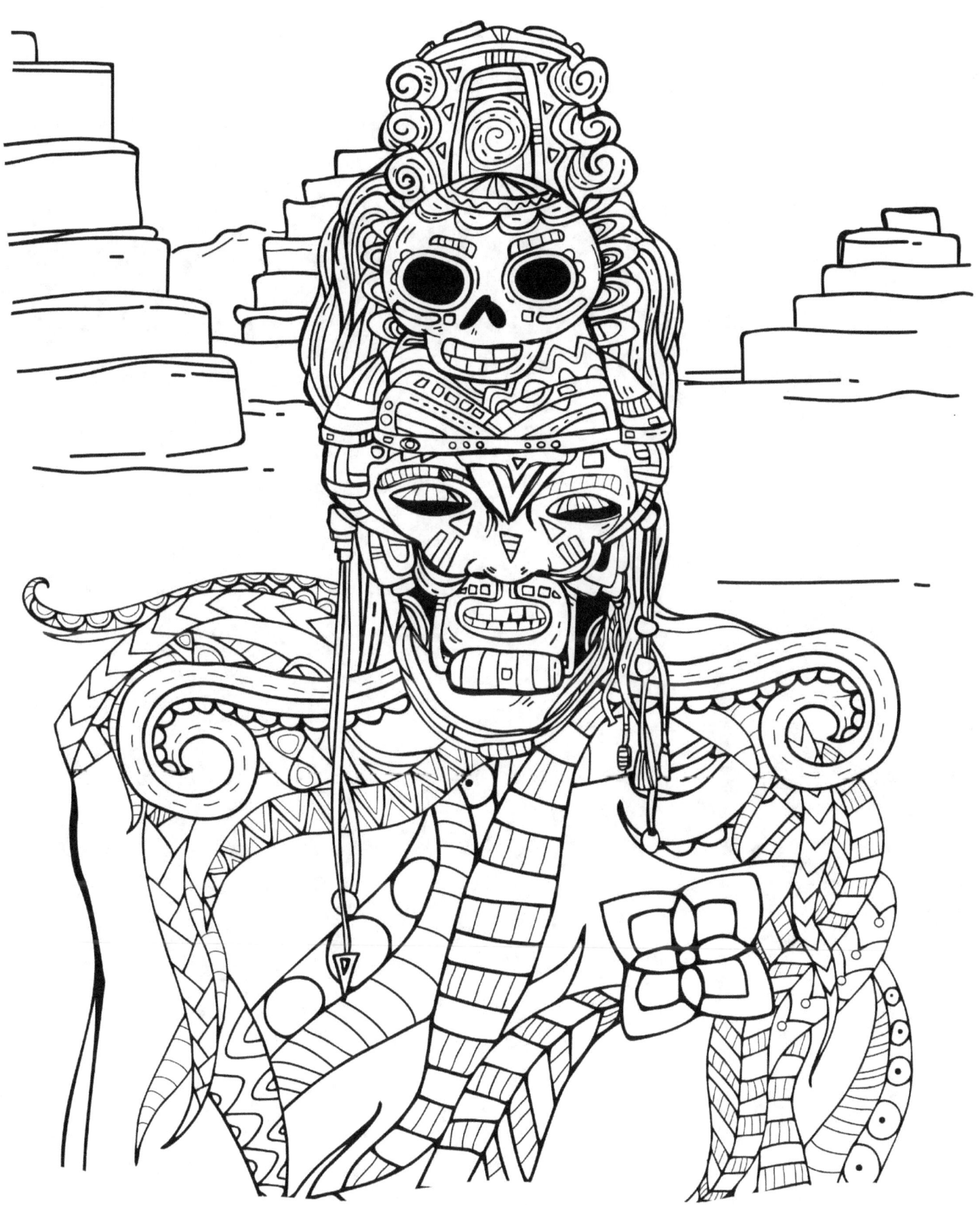

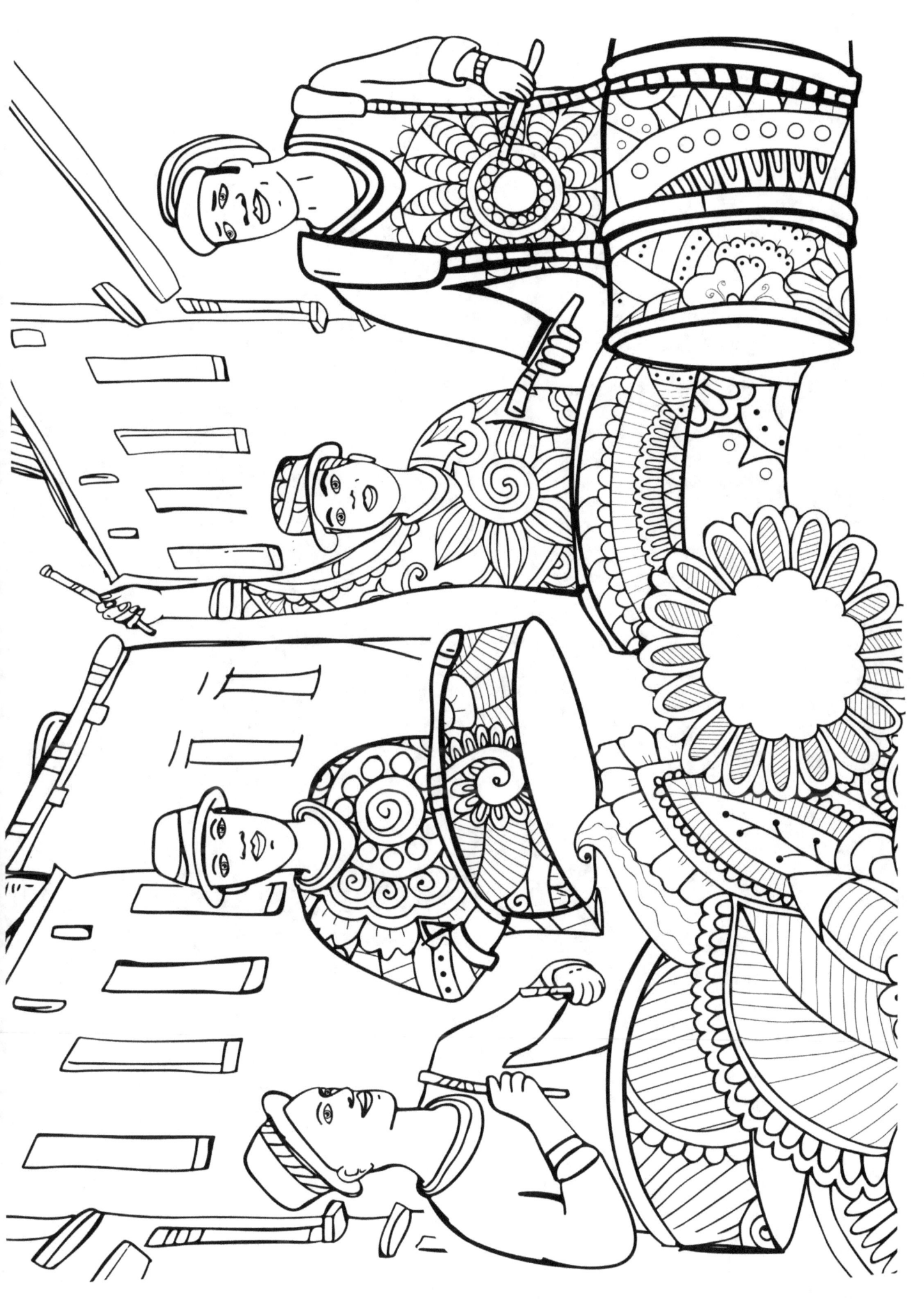

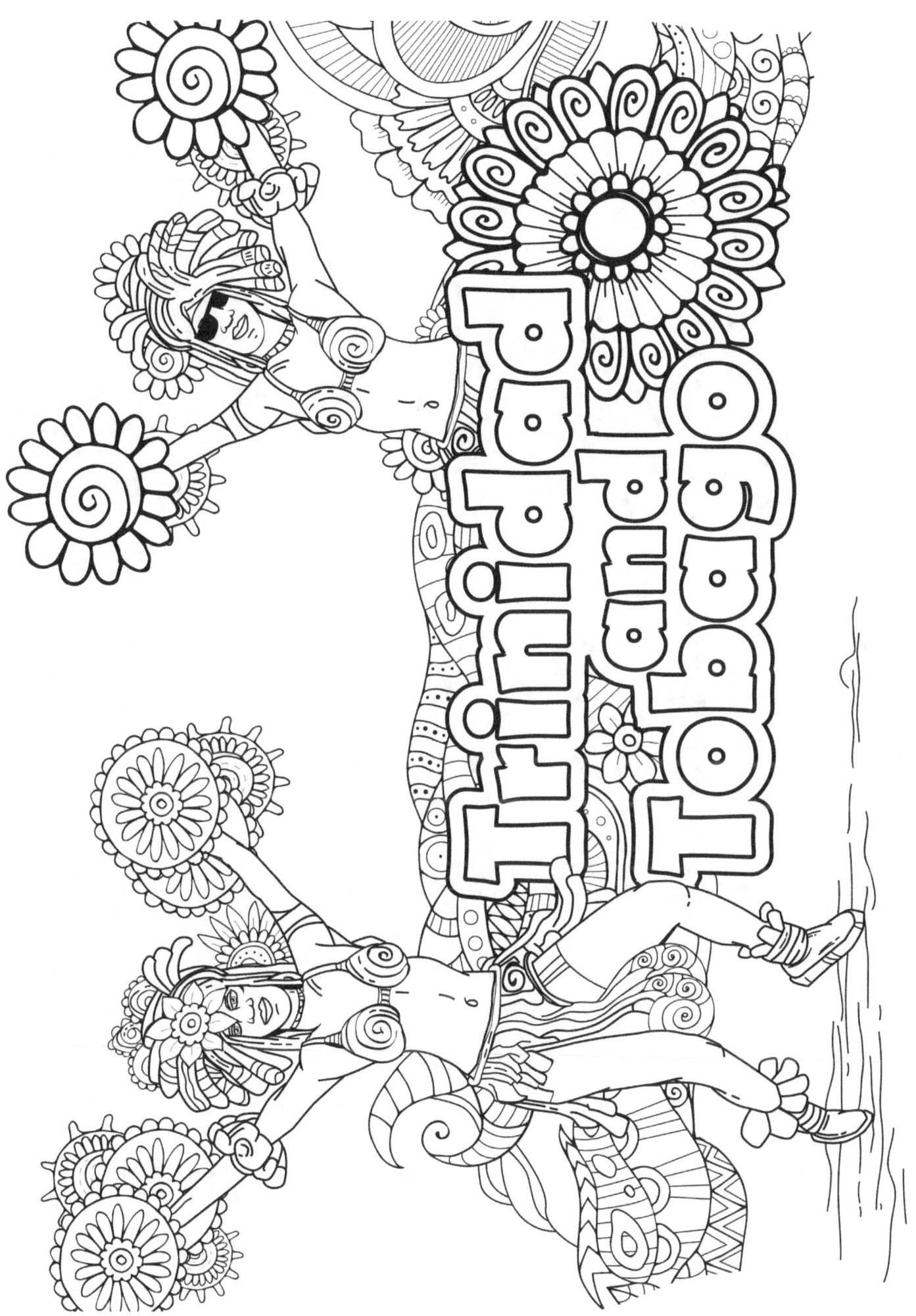

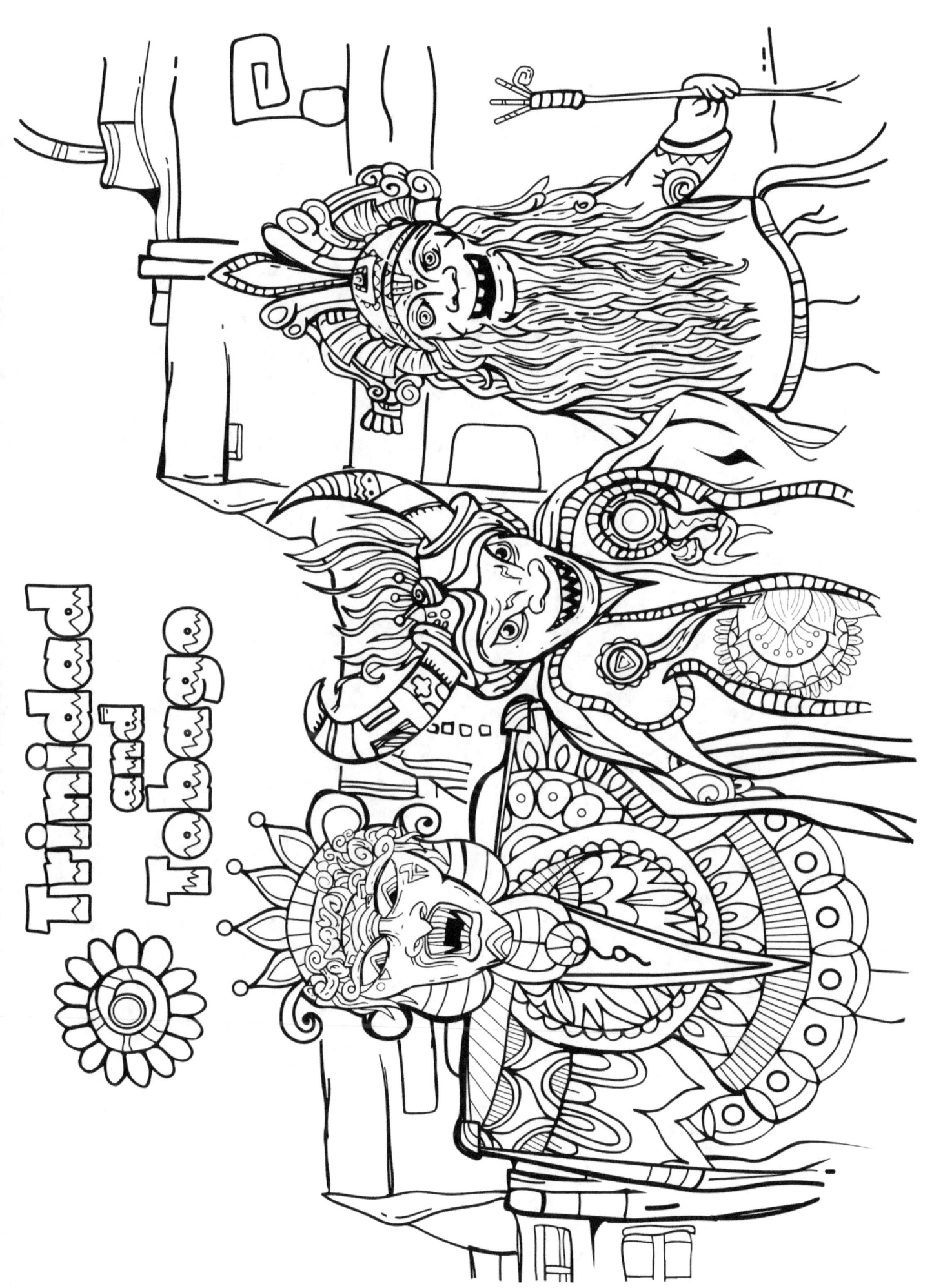

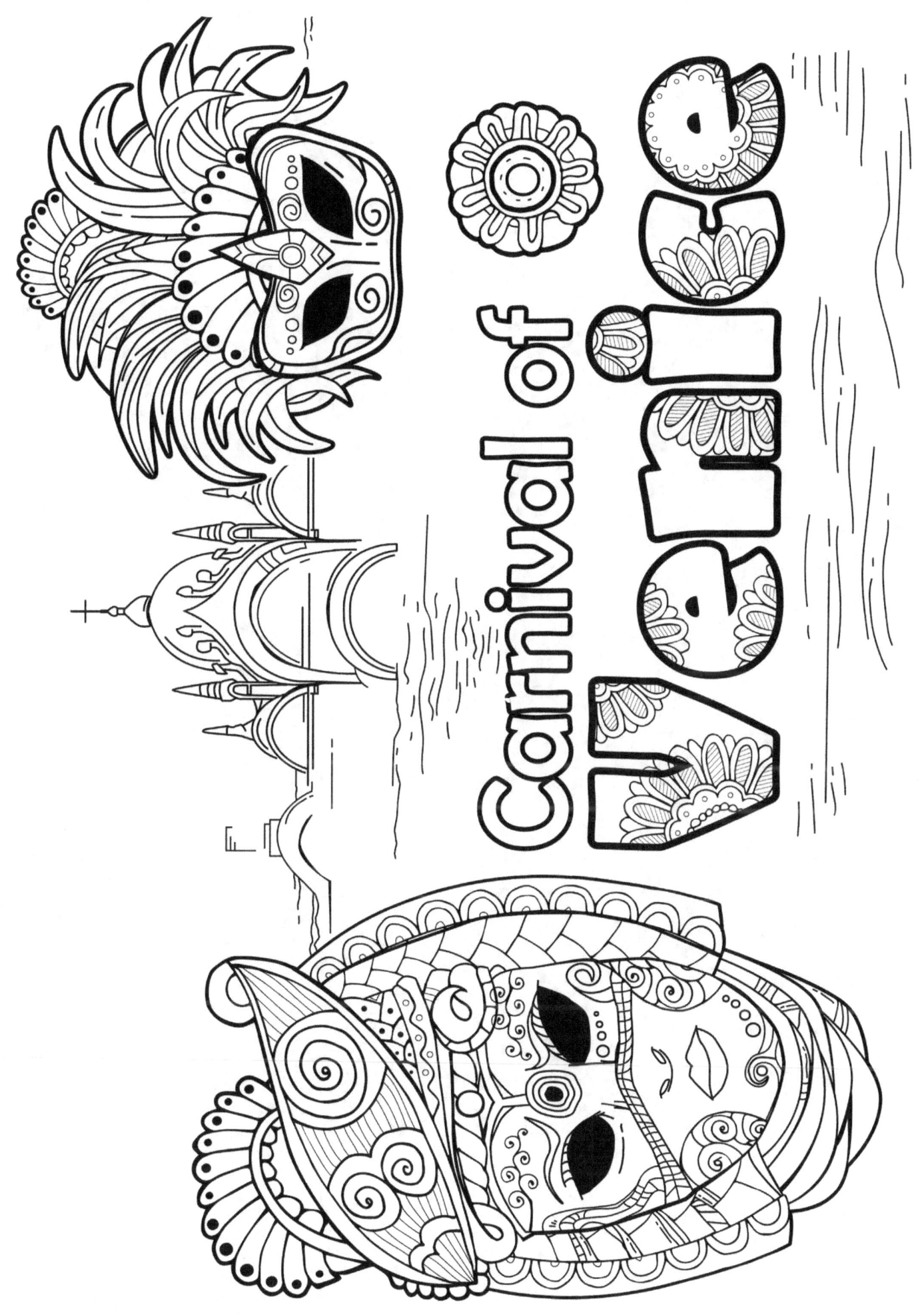

Carnival of Venice

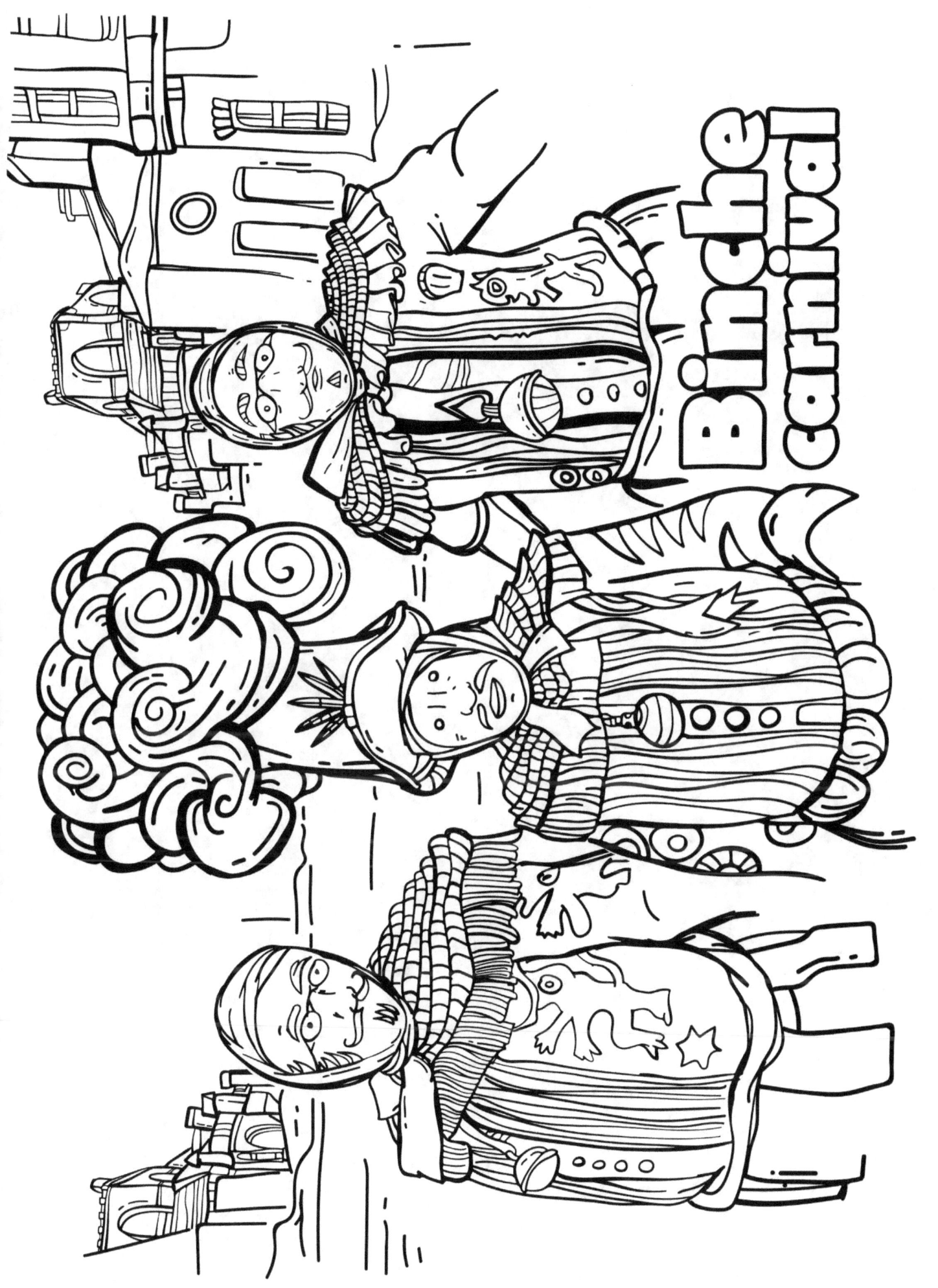

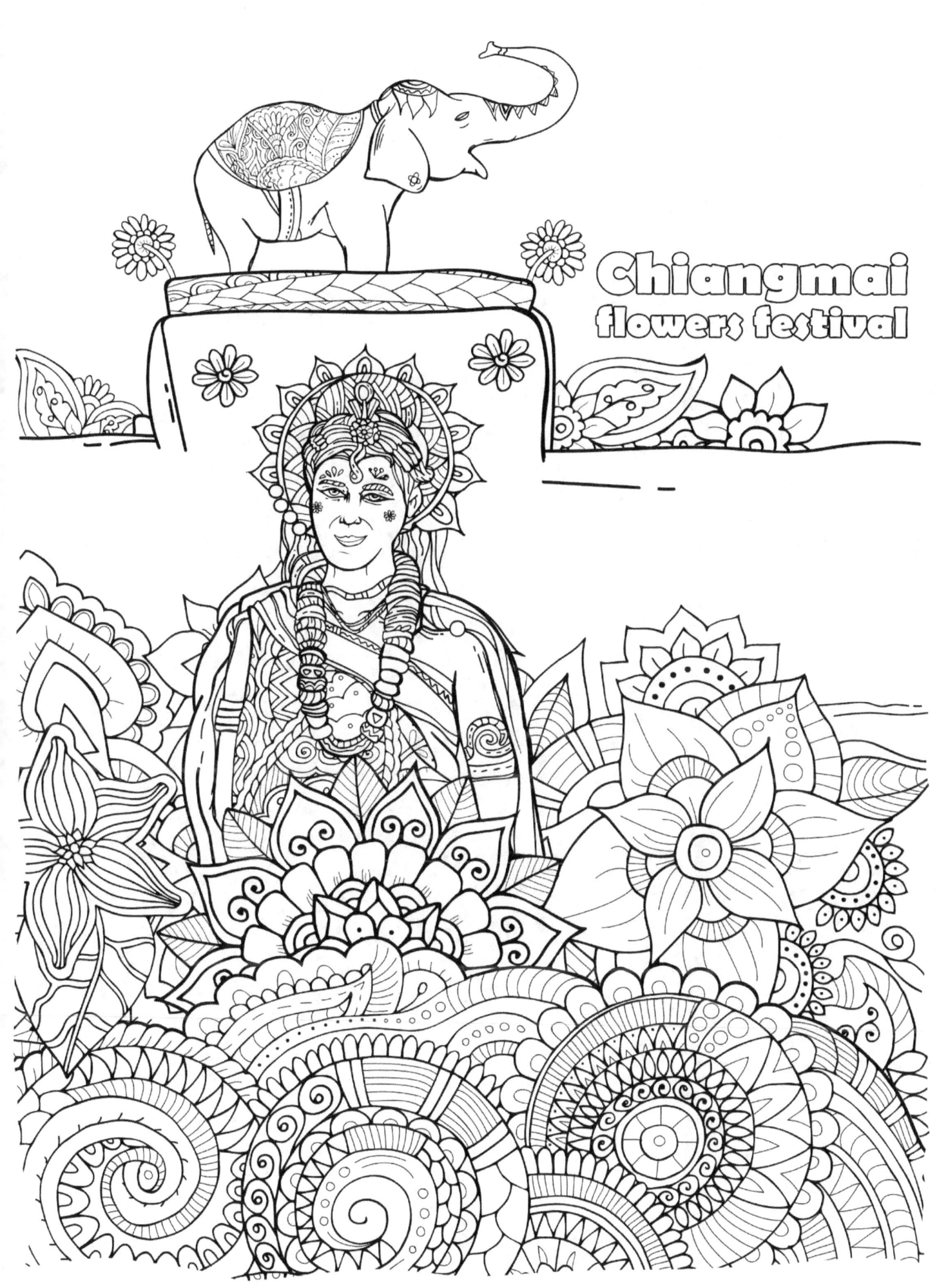

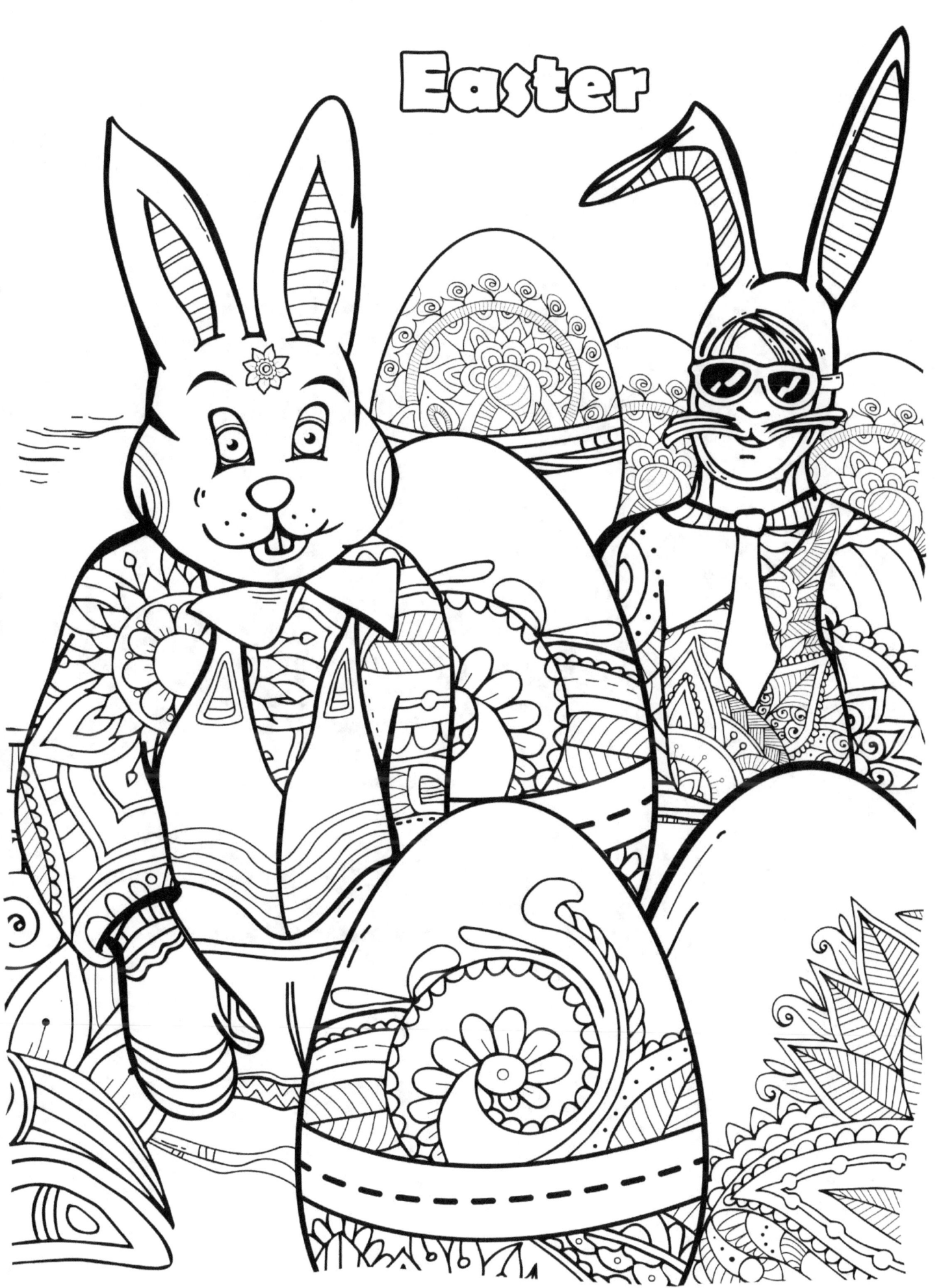

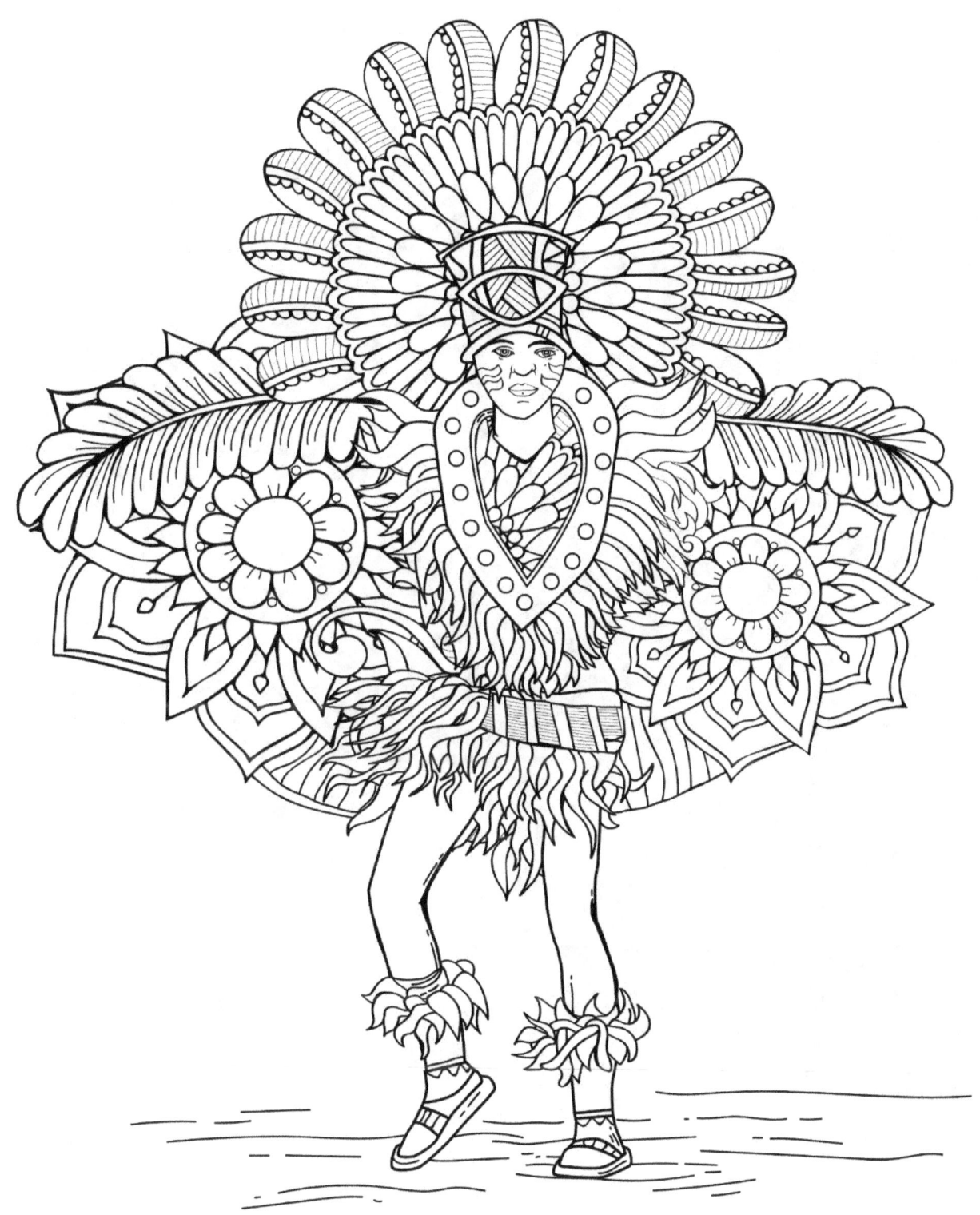

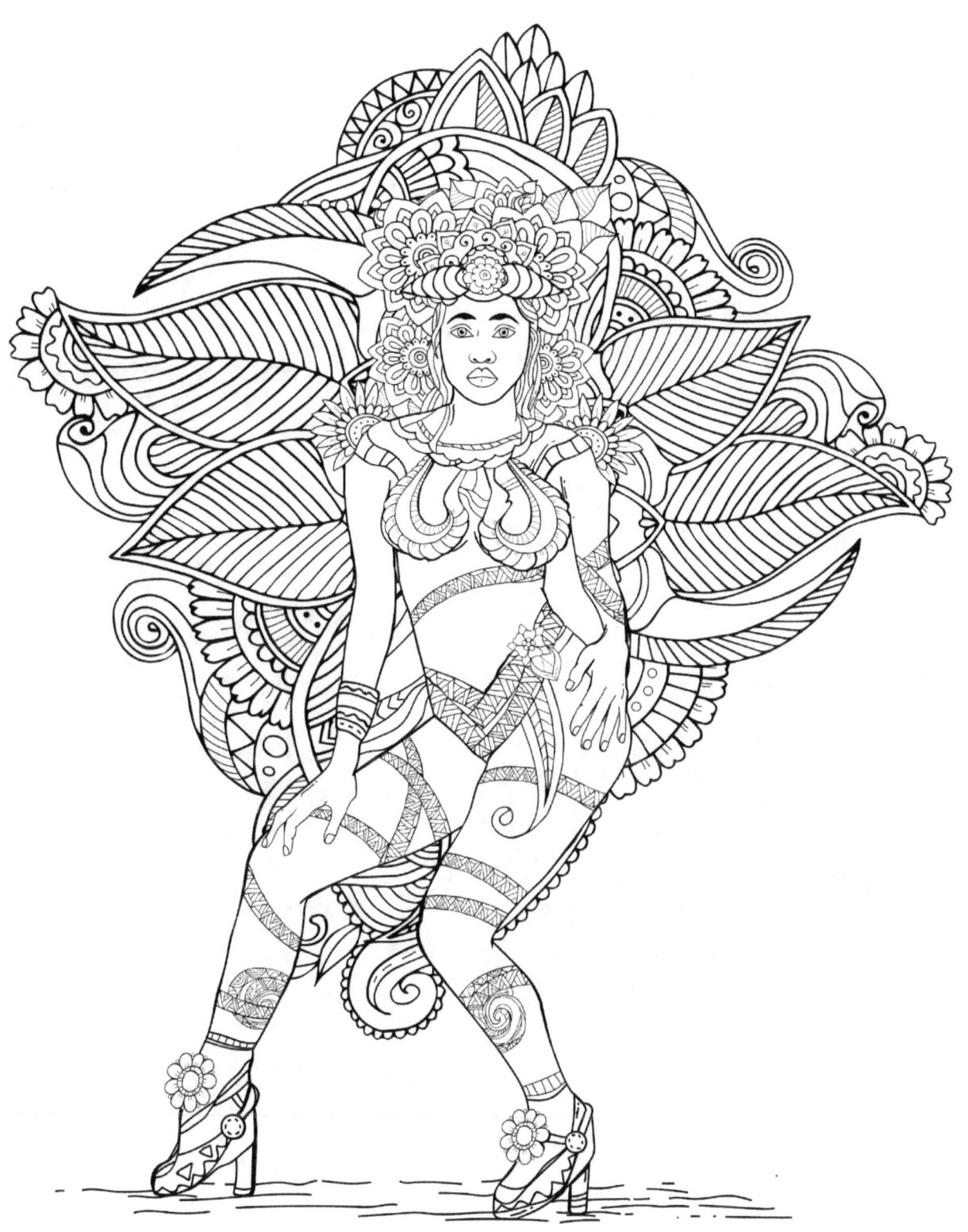

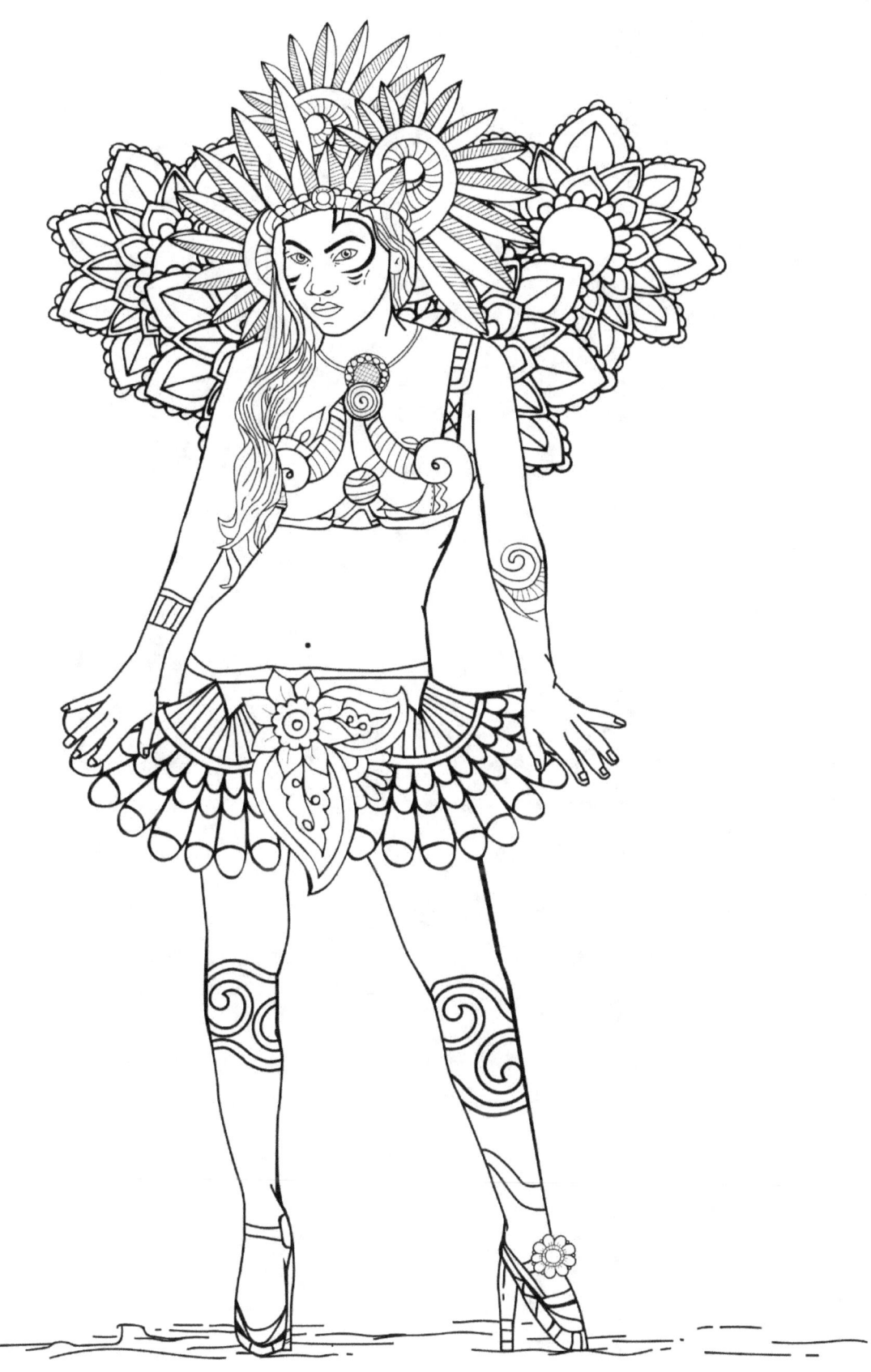

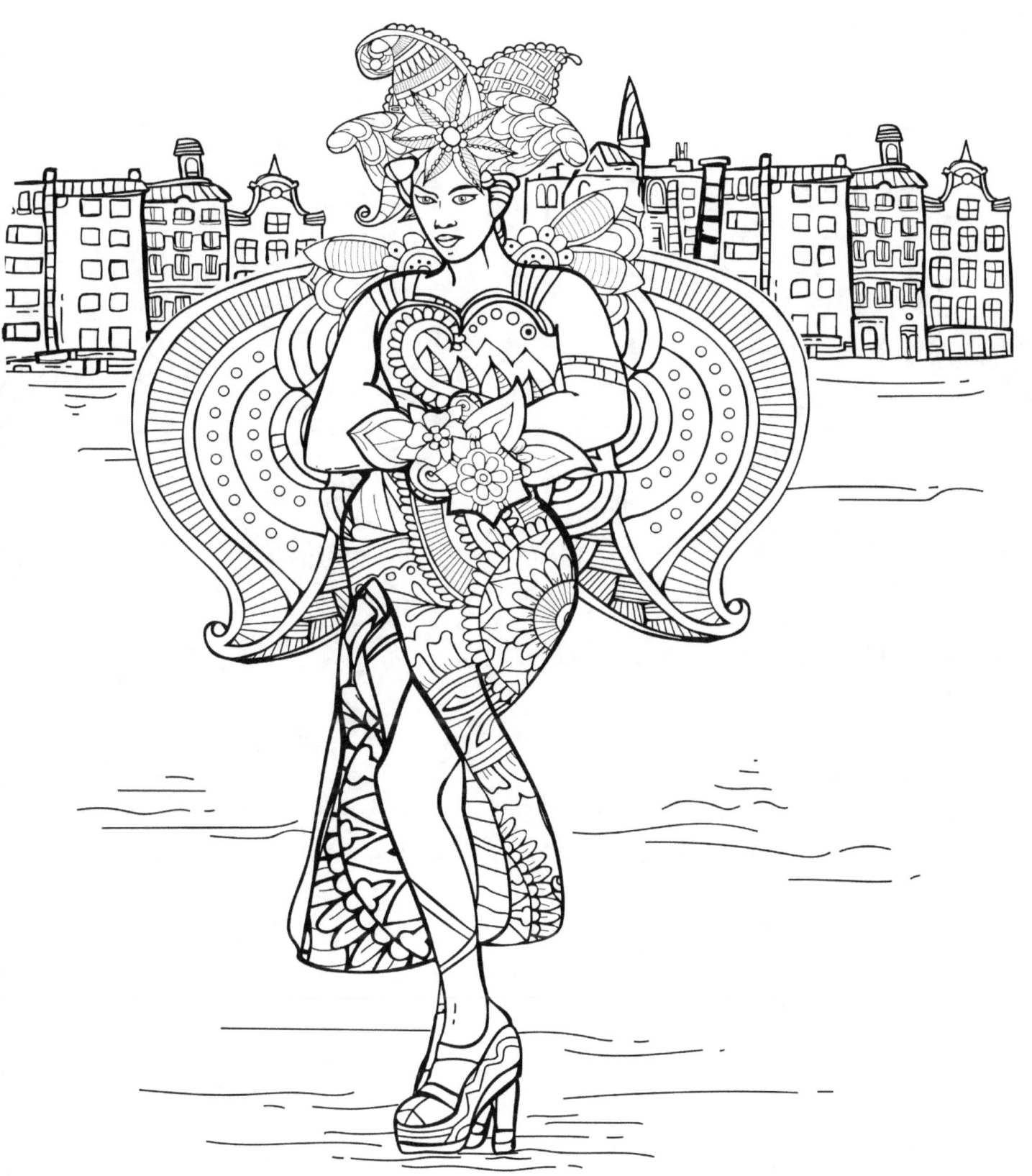

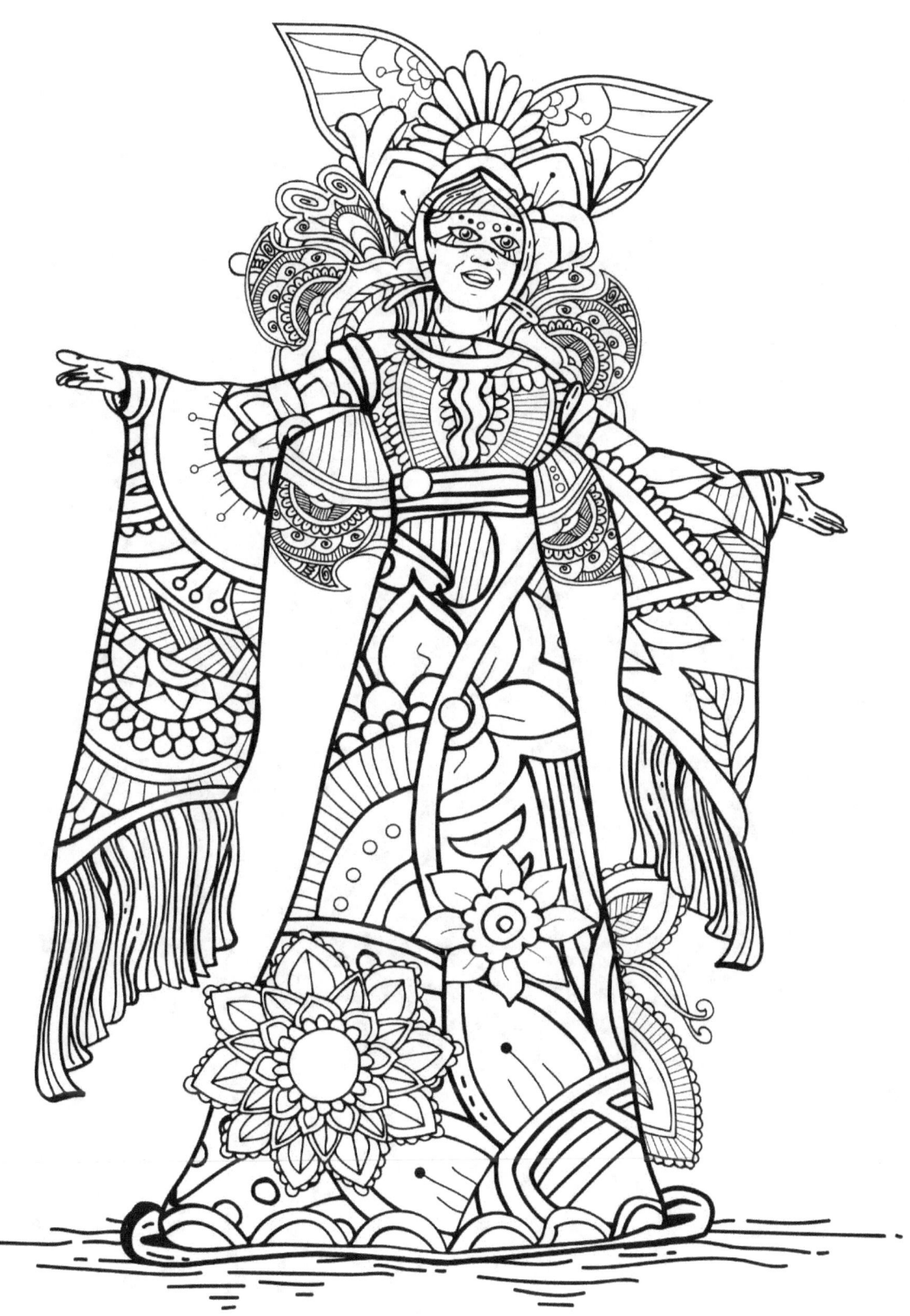

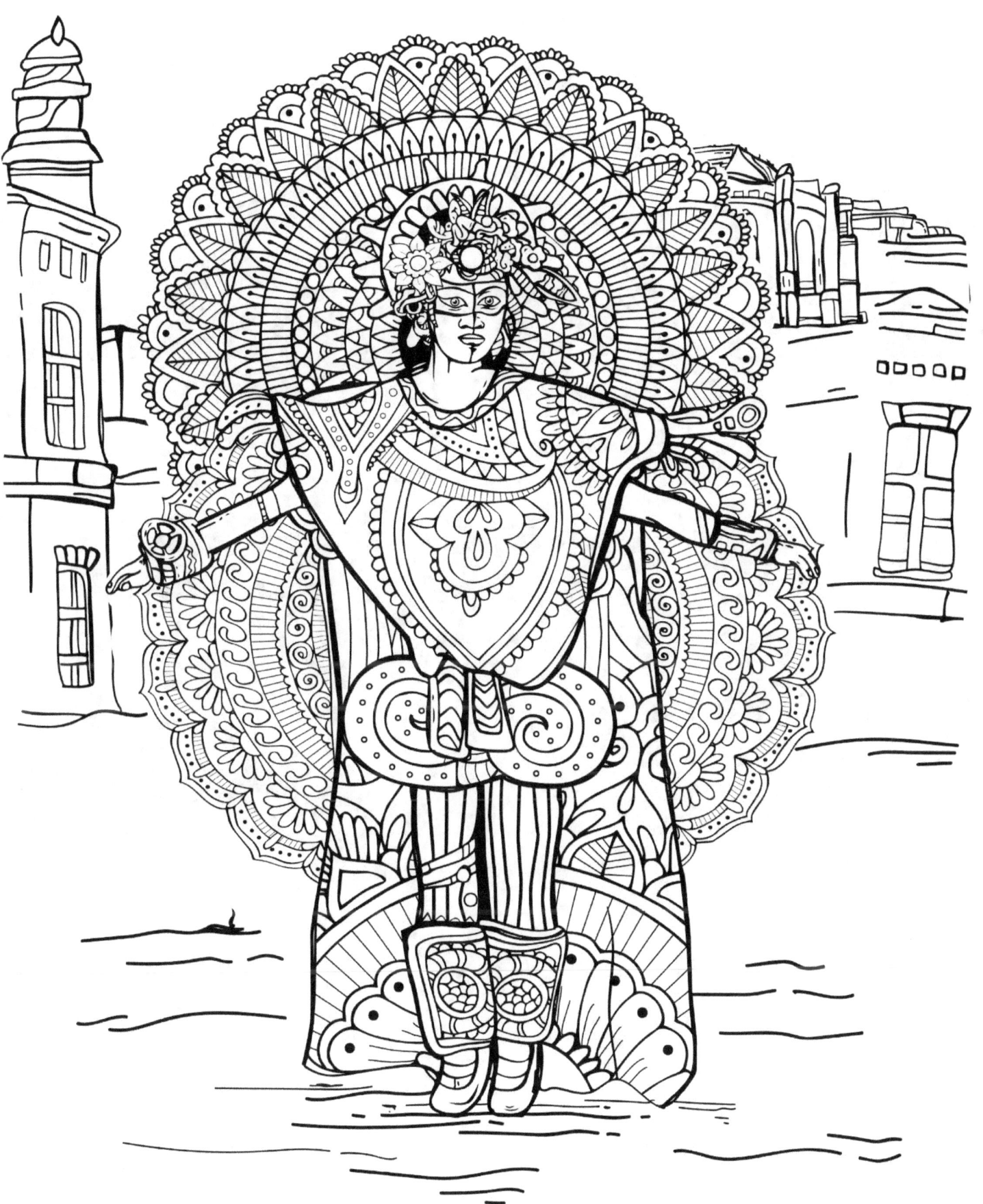

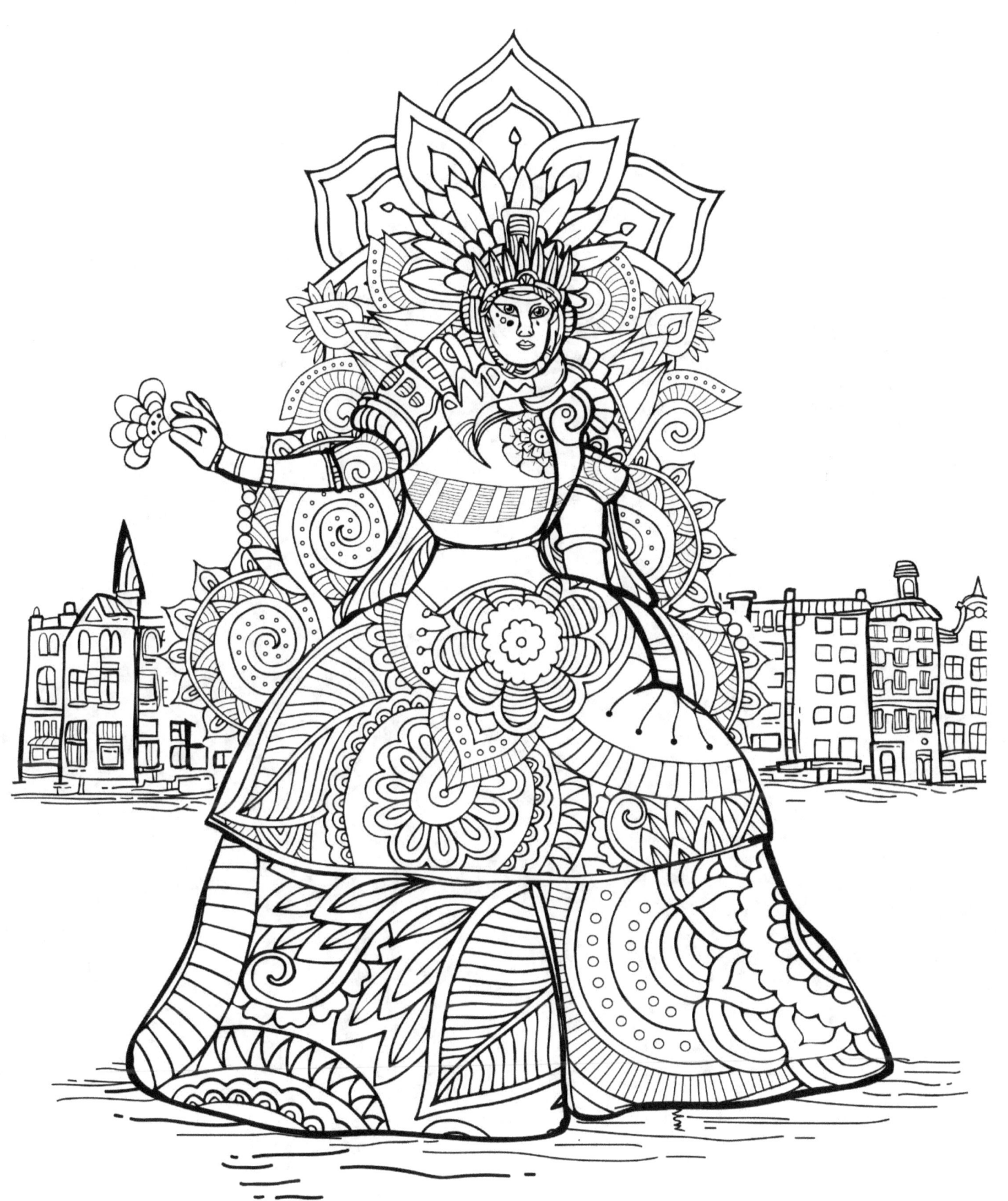

Thank you for purchasing this book.

If you would like to know more about Aryla Publishing Books please visit:-

www.ArylaPublishing.com

Or follow us on
Facebook
Twitter
Instagram
for *free promotions*

@arylapublishing

We would love to know what you think of this book so please leave us a review.

Have a wonderful day ☺

Other Coloring Books from Aryla Publishing

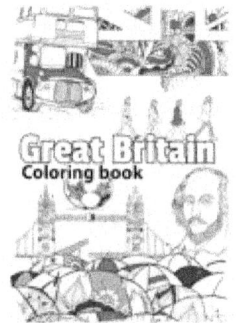
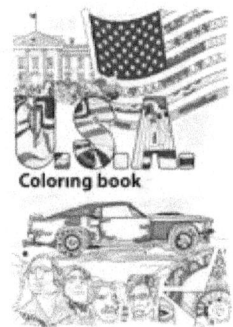
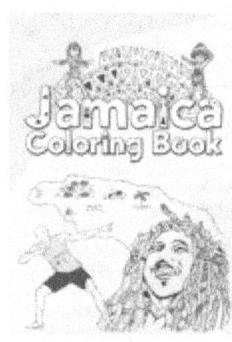
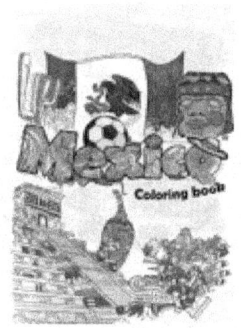
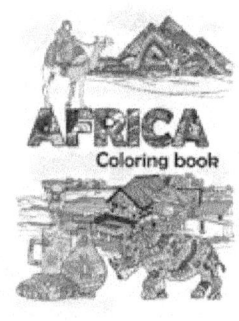

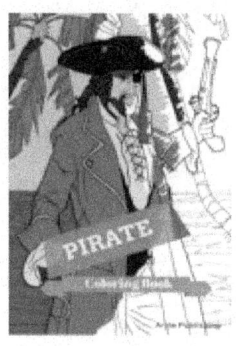
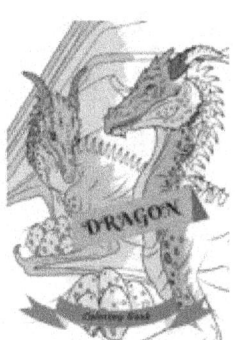
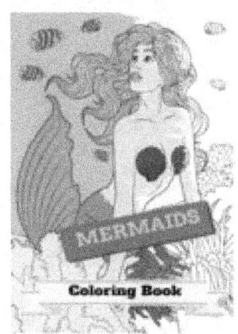
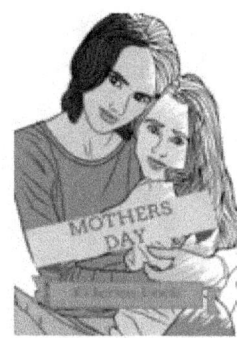
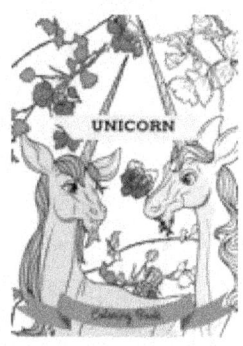

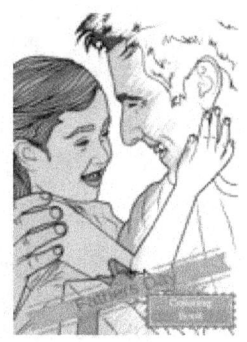

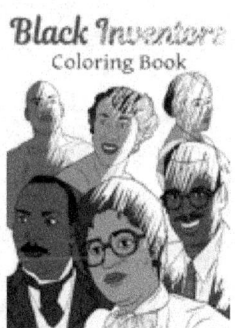
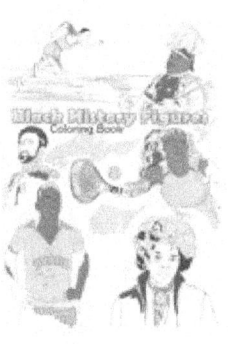

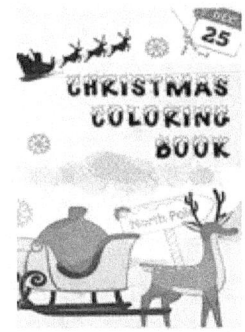
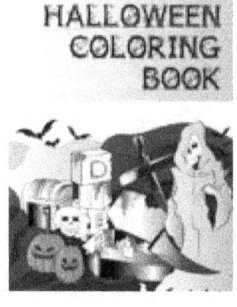
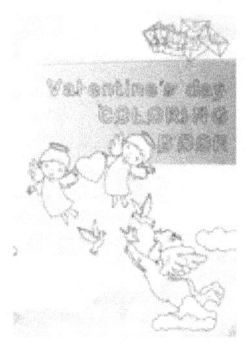
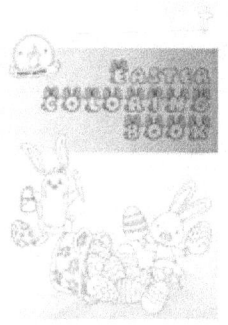